THE FELLOWSHIP OF THE CRAFT

Kennikat Press
National University Publications
Literary Criticism Series

General Editor
John E. Becker
Fairleigh Dickinson University

C. F. BURGESS

THE FELLOWSHIP
OF THE CRAFT

Conrad on
Ships and Seamen and the Sea

National University Publications
KENNIKAT PRESS   //   1976
Port Washington, N. Y.   //   London

Manufactured in the United States of America

Published by
Kennikat Press Corp.
Port Washington, N.Y. / London

Library of Congress Cataloging in Publication Data

Burgess, Chester Francis.
    The fellowship of the craft.

    (Literary criticism series) (National
university publications)
    Includes index.
    1. Conrad, Joseph, 1857-1924—Criticism and
interpretation. 2. Sea in literature. I. Title.
PR6005.04Z568   823'.9'12   75-31644
ISBN 0-8046-9116-9

FOR "BOU,"
WHO NEVER COMPLAINED DURING THE THREE YEARS
CONRAD LIVED WITH US.

CONTENTS

PREFACE

Critical interest in Conrad has followed an ascending curve in the past twenty-five years. So too has the quality of the numerous critical studies which this interest has generated.

In the first quarter-century following his death in 1924, however, Conrad suffered what appears to be the common lot of creative artists of any stature who have just passed from the scene: he became the subject of a spate of personal reminiscences, of "As-I-Remember-Him" books. (See Hemingway for the most recent manifestation of this recurring syndrome.)

In Conrad's case these early books, by his family, friends and acquaintances, are no better nor worse than any other volumes in this genre. Books such as Ford Madox Ford's *Joseph Conrad: A Personal Remembrance,* or Richard Curle's *The Last Twelve Years of Joseph Conrad,* or Jessie Conrad's *Joseph Conrad as I Knew Him* are all pleasant, noncontroversial and mildly informative. The defects of these works are self-evident: either the writer keeps getting in the way of his subject, as is the case with Ford; or the writer stops just this side of outright idolatry, as is the case with Curle; or the writer has, in fact, very little to say, as is the case with Mrs. Conrad. Over and above these specific shortcomings, these early pieces of Conradiana share one major flaw—a lack of perspective. In each instance the observers have been in too close proximity to their subject and are victims of a critical disorientation brought on by the impact of actually knowing an authentic genius.

The pioneer work in the way of objective, balanced, thoroughly researched and thoroughly documented Conrad studies came in 1940 with John Dozier Gordan's *Joseph Conrad: The Making of a Novelist.* And after Gordan, the critical floodgates opened. In the second quarter-century since Conrad's death, Conrad studies have proliferated, and in the last fifteen years of this period not a single year has passed that did not mark the advent of another book on Conrad. Of the more general studies, the best biography is Jocelyn Baines's *Joseph Conrad: A Critical Biography,* and the best overall critical work is Albert J. Guerard's *Conrad the Novelist.* But general studies, either essentially biographical or essentially critical, form only a modest portion of the Conrad critical canon. Highly specialized works have also appeared, and in abundance. There are, for example, studies of Conrad as political theorist, such as Eloise Knapp Hay's *The Political Novels of Joseph Conrad,* and Norman Sherry's two volumes devoted to fixing the *données* for many of Conrad's people and places, *Conrad's Eastern World* and its companion *Conrad's Western World.* There have been examinations of Conrad's Slavic heritage, such as Zladislaw Najder's *Conrad's Polish Background;* psychological studies such as Dr. Bernard C. Meyer's *Joseph Conrad: A Psychoanalytical Biography;* studies of Conrad's imagery, such as Ted Eugene Boyle's *Symbol and Meaning in the Fiction of Joseph Conrad;* studies of Conrad as moralist, such as Paul L. Wiley's *Conrad's Measure of Man;* and studies concentrating on the shorter tales only, such as Lawrence Graver's *Conrad's Short Fiction.*

It would appear that every approach to, every phase of, and every nuance of Conrad and his art have been examined in detail sufficient to satisfy, if not sate, the most demanding of his readers or critics. Why, then, another book on Conrad?

Because a significant area of investigation has been unexplored. Despite the wide range of approaches and emphases to be found in recent writings on Conrad, all of them, in greater or lesser degree, raise one issue in common, Conrad's relation to the sea. But, having raised the issue, most of Conrad's critics give it no more than passing and cursory attention; in the main they are content to mouth the commonplace generalizations that Conrad loved the sea and ships and was convinced that the seaman's calling was the best possible way of life. Even studies which focus directly on Conrad the seaman, such as Jerry Allen's *The Sea Years of Joseph Conrad* and G. Jean-Aubry's *The Sea Dreamer*, accept these generalizations and devote their energies to retracing Conrad's voyages and to identifying the ships he sailed on and the men he sailed with.

No writer on Conrad has ever tested the truth of these generalizations. No writer on Conrad has ever taken a close, intent look at Conrad's writings in an effort to determine *exactly* what Conrad thought or felt about the sea, about ships, about men who go to sea and about the subtle, unspoken and unseen tie which binds all worthy seamen in what Conrad calls "the fellowship of the craft." This book proposes to take just such a close and intent look and to put the generalizations to the test, using the explicit evidence provided by Conrad's two autobiographical memoirs, *The Mirror of the Sea* and *A Personal Record*, and the wealth of implicit evidence to be found in the sea tales. In such a pursuit, five areas of consideration naturally present themselves and provide convenient chapter divisions: Conrad, the seaman, speaking of the land, of the sea, of ships, of the "craft," and of seamen.

On the matter of which of Conrad's works are and are not sea tales, I have been extremely arbitrary. Some readers, for example, may be distressed to find that I have omitted *Nostromo*. My reply is that, despite the novel's coastal setting and a capataz de cargadores as central character, *Nostromo*'s chief concern is not with the sea but with man as a political animal and with the nobility and corruptibility of human nature. Other readers may be surprised to find that I have included *Heart of Darkness*. They should not be. Marlow's African adventure qualifies as a sea tale in a number of ways, but especially in a way that is crucial for the central thesis of this book. For, it is in the Marlow stories, with Marlow as spokesman, that Conrad seems best able to distill the wisdom he had acquired in the two decades he devoted to the sea. It is through Marlow as spokesman that we can best hear Joseph Conrad giving us his impressions and his judgments of the seas he had sailed, of the ships he had known, and of the men who shared with him his chancey and lonely calling. And it is precisely these impressions and these judgments that this study seeks to extract.

I am indebted to Commander Edward Frothingham, Jr., U.S.N. (Retd.), for his advice on matters technical; to Karen Frishkoff for her excellent and painstaking advice on matters editorial; and to my colleague, Dr. Lloyd J. Davidson, for his wisdom on matters literary. Finally, my thanks to Dr. George L. Roth, Jr., for creating time for Conrad.

The Virginia Military Institute
Lexington, Virginia

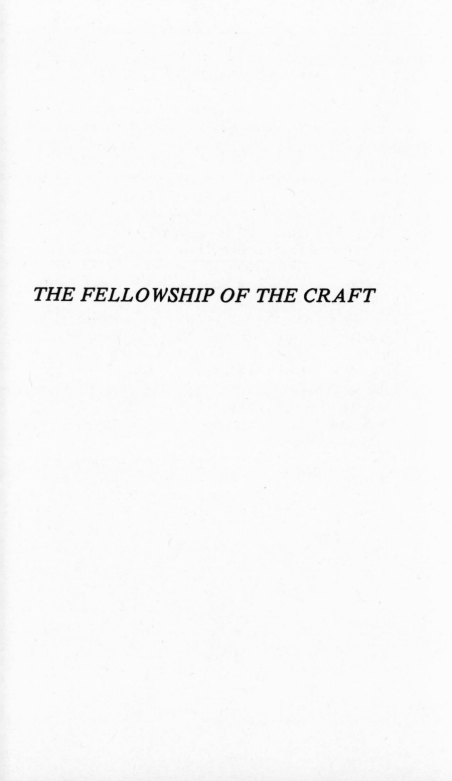

THE FELLOWSHIP OF THE CRAFT

LIST OF CONRAD TEXTS CITED

Almayer's Folly. New York: Doubleday, Page & Company, 1925.

An Outcast of the Islands. New York: Doubleday, Page & Company, 1925.

A Personal Record. New York: Harper & Brothers, 1912.

Heart of Darkness (Norton Critical Edition, ed. Robert Kimbrough). New York: W. W. Norton & Company, 1971.

Lord Jim (Norton Critical Edition, ed. Thomas C. Moser). New York: W. W. Norton & Company, 1968.

The End of the Tether in *Joseph Conrad, Tales of Land and Sea.* New York: Hanover House, 1953.

The Mirror of the Sea. New York: Doubleday, Page & Company, 1925.

The Nigger of the "Narcissus" in *The Portable Conrad,* ed. Morton Dauwen Zabel. New York: The Viking Press, 1968.

The Rescue: A Romance of the Shallows (The Norton Library). New York: W. W. Norton & Company, 1968.

"The Secret Sharer" in *The Portable Conrad,* ed. Morton Dauwen Zabel. New York: The Viking Press, 1968.

The Shadow-Line: A Confession. New York: Doubleday, Page & Company, 1925.

Typhoon and Other Stories. New York: Doubleday, Page & Company, 1925.

"Youth" in *The Portable Conrad,* ed. Morton Dauwen Zabel. New York: The Viking Press, 1968.

CHAPTER ONE

THE LAND

The lagoon, the beach, the colors and the shapes struck her more than ever as a luminous painting. —*The Rescue*

A Landfall may be good or bad. —*The Mirror of the Sea*

. . . they would be together on the great blue sea that was like life—away from the forests that were like death.
—*Almayer's Folly*

In *An Outcast of the Islands,* Tom Lingard assures the youthful Willems that "there's only one place for an honest man. The sea, my boy, the sea!" (p. 42). The remark is not particularly striking in its originality, nor is it a prime candidate for use as yet another apt Conradian epigraph. What is striking about Lingard's observation is how few of Conrad's seamen, honest men in the main, follow this stricture, how few devote themselves to the sea fully and as far as it is possible to do so escape the land.

In fact, among all the men of the sea who people Conrad's pages, those who have broken free of the land comprise a small group indeed, numbering exactly three. There is, first of all and preeminently, the venerable Singleton, the oldest able seaman aboard the *Narcissus,* who, by the reckoning of his shipmates, has spent something less than one-tenth of his adult life on land. Singleton's knowledge of the world ashore has been acquired, presumably, by means of vicarious experience from such books as Bulwer-Lytton's *Pelham,* a fact which boggles the mind of the narrator of *The Nigger of the "Narcissus".* But Singleton's knowledge of the sea and of ships is encyclopedic and his judgment on nautical matters is authoritative.

3

Second in this select trio of totally committed seafarers is Carter, the mate of the yacht *Hermit* in *The Rescue*. By the testimony of no less an expert witness than Lingard himself, Carter conducts himself "like a seaman" (p. 329), though, ironically, his exemplary action proves disastrous for Lingard. And Carter unhesitatingly gives up the amenities of the pleasure yacht, under whose easygoing regimen he chafes, to follow Lingard to whatever seaway the call of adventure and the brig *Lightning* may bring them.

Finally, there is Mr. Baker, whom Conrad (or, more precisely, the narrator of *The Nigger of the "Narcissus")* terms "a model chief mate" (p. 447). And so he is, and chiefly because all of his energies, personal and professional, are dedicated to the sea and, most especially, to his ship. It is Baker who, in the midst of the gale, berates the fractious crew of the *Narcissus* by reminding them that they are not passengers. Baker's simple and straightforward credo is that "We are here to take care of the ship" (p. 364) and the crew are so informed in no-nonsense terms. The degree of Baker's isolation from the land is perhaps best revealed in one of the most poignant episodes in the novel, the scene in which Baker sits alone on the deck of the deserted *Narcissus,* now safely berthed in a London dock. "He didn't like to part with a ship," we are told by the narrator (p. 447) and this is no doubt true, but what is equally true is that, in the whole of his native England, there is absolutely no place for Baker to go.

The catalogue of Conrad's sailors who preserve ties ashore is, on the other hand, both impressive and lengthy. Some of these ties are admittedly slight and in the normal run of things. Solomon Rout, for instance, of the steamship *Nan-Shan,* in *Typhoon,* "good man" and dedicated ship's engineer though he may be, derives his chief pleasure from the lively correspondence he maintains with his agreeable wife back in the "little cottage near Teddington" (p. 15); the master of the *Nan-Shan,* Captain MacWhirr, is also a letter writer, although his logbook-like missives go largely unappreciated by the "quite superior" lady, his wife, to whom they are addressed; Creighton, the vigorous second mate of the *Narcissus,* indulges, in an idle moment, in harmless dreams of a "long country lane . . . the caressing blueness of an English sky . . . a girl in a clear dress, smiling under a sunshade" (p. 310), while his equally vigorous skipper, Captain Allistoun, wants nothing more from life than to end his days "in a little house, with a plot of ground attached—far in the country—out of sight of the sea" (p. 319); Podmore, the would-be redeemer of souls and cook extraordinary of the *Narcissus,* never forgets the evangelical mission which awaits him at home, although he is able to bring the good news to his family but one month in twelve; Jörgenson, erstwhile freewheeling adventurer and skipper of the bark *Wild Rose,* settles down with the woman who came "by way of exchange for a lot of cotton stuffs and several brass guns" (*The Rescue,* p. 389), and he joins Lingard in the abortive attempt to restore Hassim to power only on Lingard's promise to remember that "the girl must eat" (p. 104).

Some of the ties to land are less innocuous, however, and succeed in compromising the seaman's effectiveness and his judgment. Captain Beard, the admirable master of Marlow's first Eastern-going ship, the *Judea,* in "Youth," is discomfited to find that, in a moment of crisis, his concern for his wife's safety is greater than his concern for the welfare of his ship; Captain Archbold, of the ill-fated *Sephora* in "The Secret Sharer," has his wife on board too, as he announces on every possible occasion, and his otherwise inane iteration of this fact seems to reflect the degree of irregularity involved in his effort to reconcile his domestic obligations with his duty to his ship; Captain Whalley, in *The End of the Tether,* is committed to the degrading and irksome task of piloting the disreputable *Sofala* in its tedious rounds of forgotten ports of call (hardly an appropriate undertaking for the discoverer of Whalley Passage) in order to support his widowed daughter in Melbourne. And sometimes these ties with the land can compromise an entire ship. In *The Rescue,* for instance, the adventurous Carter is thus contemptuous of the crew of the pleasure yacht, *Hermit:* "Every man jack of them has a petticoat in tow" (p. 193). Of their elaborate bedding, Carter is equally scornful: " . . . they mean to sleep soft—and dream of home—maybe. Home. Think of that" (p. 194).

In some instances, the ties with the land can be fatal. Jim is very much aware of the parsonage in Essex from which he came and to which he can never return, and his ultimate commitment and his ultimate test, which end disastrously, come on land, in Patusan. And ironically, it is Tom Lingard, the so-called King of the Sea, the man who would have all good sailors at sea, who is bound most fast and most fundamentally to the land. At different times in his career, in *Almayer's Folly, An Outcast of the Islands* and *The Rescue,* he assumes direct responsibility for the welfare of the orphan, Nina, of his luckless son-in-law, Almayer, of Willems, of Hassim, of Immada, of Jörgenson, of Belarab, of the Shore of Refuge, of the settlement on the Pantai, of the entire Wajo people; and, without exception, Lingard's commitments ashore end in failure.

There remains to be considered Conrad's favorite seaman, the garrulous Charlie Marlow. For Marlow we must create a special category, since, just as he is both in and out of the stories he tells, so too Marlow is both of the sea and of the land. Conrad's agent and alter ego, as his creator did, lives in both worlds, interpreting the sea for those who know it only by the view from the shore and, at the same time, bringing to the sea a wide experience gained ashore.

The ambivalence of Marlow's position can be readily seen by referring to the sketchy but revealing biography of the seaman cum storyteller provided in *Heart of Darkness.* Here we are told that one way in which Marlow is not representative of his class is that he has a proclivity for seeking out associations and experiences on shore. In Conrad's words, Marlow was indeed a thoroughgoing seaman "but he was a wanderer too" (p. 5). Unlike his colleagues before the mast, Marlow is not one of the "stay-at-home" cast who, after a casual spree ashore, return to the ship and remain disdainfully ignorant of "the foreign shores, the foreign faces, the changing immensity of life" (p. 5). (In point of fact, on the face of the evidence already gleaned from Conrad, the average seaman is not *all* that committed to the ship—his home, and to the sea—his country.) Marlow, then, like so many of Conrad's seamen, has strong ties with the land.

Yet, of the five men who occasionally share an after-dinner

cheroot, a bottle, and their memories of days and nights on the
bridge, it is Marlow alone who still follows the sea. Only Marlow
remains committed to the manage of ships and to the mysteries
of the deep, and he alone has resisted the blandishments of two
good addresses, a butcher round one corner, a policeman round
another, and a normal temperature year-round. Marlow is, in
fact, a bit smug on the subject, seldom missing an opportunity
to remind his auditors of his fidelity to the sea. It is this duality,
this capacity for functioning in both worlds, which enables Marlow to survive, ashore and at sea. It is also this duality which
enables Marlow to avoid some of the mistakes of his less informed and less resilient peers—a point that will be of some
importance in a later chapter.

There are, of course, certain ties with the land which no
seaman, no matter how dedicated to the craft, no matter how
committed to the sea, can avoid. To put the matter in its simplest
terms, every voyage at sea is a progression from one point of
land to another point of land, and a ship is always heading on a
fixed course for a fixed destination on land. Thus, at two points
in every passage the seaman cannot escape the land.

In *The Mirror of the Sea* (p. 3), Conrad underscores this
polarity as follows: "Landfall and Departure mark the rhythmical swing of a seaman's life and of a ship's career. From land
to land is the most concise definition of a ship's earthly fate."
He goes on (pp. 3–5) to describe the excitement and the bustle
attendant on the weighing of the anchor and, at the other pole,
the increased tempo aboard ship from the first cry of "Land ho"
to the final order, always given by the chief mate, "Let go." Departure and landfall are, in Conrad's mind, the climactic points
of any voyage, and they both involve the ship and the land rather
than the ship and the sea.

"A Departure," says Conrad (p. 4), "the last professional
sight of land, is always good, or at least good enough." Conrad
is speaking from a technical point of view here, since some seamen, especially ships' captains, take a departure rather badly.
Conrad recalls only one skipper who "walked his deck with a
springy step, and gave the first course of the passage in an
elated voice" (p. 5). Much more representative are the many

captains Conrad encountered who, as soon as the Channel was cleared, disappeared into their cabins for several days to reconcile themselves to the long voyage ahead and to the loss of "some affection . . . or perhaps only some pet vice" (p. 5).

On the other hand, "A Landfall may be good or bad," says Conrad (p. 4). And, again, he is speaking technically, because in at least one sense, for the seaman, all landfalls are good. The crew of the *Narcissus*, for example, gather on the forecastlehead and point excitedly at the Island of Flores in the Azores, as if it were the first land they had ever seen. It is, of course, the first they have seen in nearly four months, and the significance of the "irregular and broken outlines" (p. 426) looming before them is the proximity of land, of home, and of the end of the long and demanding voyage from Bombay to London.

Thus, the seaman's response to the leaving of and the returning to land, his sadness on leaving and his joy on returning, speak well for the appeal of land. And over and above these two emotion-charged moments, elsewhere in Conrad the land *can* present itself to the seaman's eye in a favorable, even agreeable, aspect. For example, during the long period of peace which comes when Tom Lingard establishes Belarab as ruler on the Shore of Refuge, the land undergoes a dramatic transformation. In *The Rescue*, Lingard admires the fruits of his intervention thus:

Far away the inland forests were tinted a shimmering blue, like the forests of a dream. On the seaward side the belt of great trunks and matted undergrowth came to the western shore of the oval lagoon; and in the pure freshness of the air the groups of brown houses reflected in the water or seen above the waving green of the fields, the clumps of palm trees, the fenced-in plantations, the groves of fruit trees, made up a picture of sumptuous prosperity. (p. 108)

In a similar vein, the passage of the *Narcissus* through the Channel is a visual delight for the men aboard the ship.

The clouds raced with her mastheads; they rose astern enormous and white, soared to the zenith, flew past, and falling down the wide curve of the sky seemed to dash headlong into the sea—the clouds swifter than the ship, more free, but without a home. The coast to welcome her stepped out of space into the sunshine. The

lofty headlands trod masterfully into the sea; the wide bays smiled
in the light; the shadows of homeless clouds ran along the sunny
plains, leaped over valleys, without a check darted up the hills,
rolled down the slopes; and the sunshine pursued them with patches
of running brightness. On the brows of dark cliffs white lighthouses
shone in pillars of light. The Channel glittered like a blue mantle
shot with gold and starred by the silver of the capping seas.

(pp. 442–43)

The hint of the security, of the safety provided by the land is
augmented by the contrast between the homeless clouds and the
ship nearing home.

A few moments later in *The Nigger of the "Narcissus,"*
Conrad ascends to the lyrical in celebration of his adopted home-
land. The passage, in fact, recalls the glowing terms put into the
mouth of John of Gaunt three centuries earlier by a native-born
Englishman—"this blessed plot, this earth, this realm, this England." It should be noted, however, in Conrad's tribute, that his
island home is seen, through the eyes of a seaman, as a great
ship floating timelessly and resisting the buffeting of the sea.

. . . the coast, stretching away straight and black, resembled the
high side of an indestructible craft riding motionless upon the immortal and unresting sea. The dark land lay alone in the midst of
waters, like a mighty ship bestarred with vigilant lights. . . . She
towered up immense and strong, guarding priceless traditions and
untold suffering, sheltering glorious memories and base forgetful-
ness, ignoble virtues and splendid transgressions. A great ship! . . .
A ship mother of fleets and nations! The great flagship of the race;
stronger than the storms, and anchored in the open sea. (p. 443)

Similarly, Marlow's rapturous description of his first view
of the East, in "Youth," depicts the land in most favorable
terms. It should be kept in mind, however, that this is the older
Marlow attempting to recapture the magic of that moment of
youthful exuberance and he may be guilty of some overstatement:

I see it now—the wide sweep of the bay, the glittering sands, the
wealth of green infinite and varied, the sea blue like the sea of a
dream, the crowd of attentive faces, the blaze of vivid color—the
water reflecting it all, the curve of the shore, the jetty, the high-

sterned outlandish craft floating still. . . . (pp. 152–53)

And in *Lord Jim,* Marlow speaks movingly of the seaman's
tenuous but very real ties with the land and especially of that
part of the land which is called by the name "home":

> . . . even they . . . the most free, lonely, irresponsible and bereft
> of ties,—even those for whom home holds no dear face, no familiar
> voice,--even they have to meet the spirit that dwells within the
> land, under its sky, in its air, in its valleys, and on its rises, in its
> fields, in its waters and its trees—a mute friend, judge, and inspirer.
> . . . Each blade of grass has its spot on earth whence it draws its
> life, its strength; and so is man rooted to the land from which he
> draws his faith together with his life. (pp. 135–36)

But, as has been observed earlier, Marlow is a special case.

For, despite the occasional felicitous prospect which the land
may offer the seafarer and Marlow's glowing encomium not with-
standing, the weight of the evidence in Conrad suggests that, in
the main, Lingard is right. The seaman belongs at sea, for the
land is malevolent to him in most aspects.

The malevolence of the land, when seen with the sailor's
eyes, makes its presence felt virtually whenever Conrad's seamen
near shore, and examples abound, in the sea tales, of a coast
or a shore or an inland waterway which is to be feared or re-
spected or shunned. It is this capacity of the land to be capricious
or deceitful or both that Conrad is talking about in his discussion
of good and bad landfalls in *The Mirror of the Sea.* The ship,
says Conrad (pp. 4–5), is always aiming for one particular spot
of land—"maybe a small island in the ocean, a single headland
upon the long coast of a continent, a lighthouse on a bluff . . .
if you have sighted it on the expected bearing, then that Landfall
is good." But such dead reckoning landfalls are rare; more commonly, the land plays its tricks—"Fogs, snowstorms, gales thick
with clouds and rain," and these, says Conrad, "are the enemies
of good Landfalls" (p. 5).

In *The Rescue,* the yacht *Hermit* has made a disastrous
landfall, having beached itself on the Short of Refuge. The mishap may be due in part to the inept crew, for whom Carter has
nothing but scorn, but the *Hermit*'s plight must also be attributed, in large measure, to the power of the land on that shore

to betray ships and men. The Shore of Refuge, as described by Conrad, assumes the proportions of a navigational nightmare:

Its approaches are extremely difficult for a stranger. Looked at from seaward, the innumerable islets fringing what, on account of its vast size, may be called the mainland, merge into a background that presents not a single landmark to point the way through the intricate channels. It may be said that in a belt of sea twenty miles broad along that low shore there is much more coral, mud, sand, and stones than actual sea water. (pp. 63–64)

And Mrs. Travers's first sight of the Shore of Refuge underscores the perils which this most treacherous of coasts presents to the seaman. Lingard has just told her, "This cloud is the coast and in a moment we shall be entering the creek":

Mrs. Travers stared at it. Was it land—land! It seemed to her even less palpable than a cloud, a mere sinister immobility above the unrest of the sea, nursing in its depth the unrest of men who, to her mind, were no more real than fantastic shadows. (p. 247)

Indeed, only Tom Lingard dares attempt the channels with any degree of success or safety. So too, it will be recalled, there is but one course up the River Pantai to Lingard's settlement at Sambir, a course that only Lingard knows, until Willems of *An Outcast of the Islands* betrays him and guides the Arab, Abdulla, and his ship to the settlement.

The threat, the dangers which the land poses for the safe passage of hips are, quite naturally, multiplied an hundredfold at night. In "The Secret Sharer" the young captain has committed himself, perhaps foolishly, to bringing his first command as close in as possible in order that Leggatt might have his best chance at survival. Meanwhile, the land closes in, awaiting the one mistake on the captain's part which will be fatal:

The black southern hill of Koh-ring seemed to hang right over the ship like a towering fragment of the everlasting night. On that enormous mass of blackness there was not a gleam to be seen, not a sound to be heard. It was gliding irresistibly toward us and yet seemed already within reach of the hand. (p. 695)

Indeed, in "The Secret Sharer" the clear implication is that were it not for the providential appearance of the captain's (now Leggatt's) floppy white hat as a visual marker, the land would have won out, as it usually does in such heroic but foolhardy confrontations.

Much more commonly, in Conrad, the land presents no particular problems in seamanship, but the threat is still there and it is still felt by the seaman. On these occasions, the land looms as a menacing, insidious, and immutable presence. Marlow's description of the African coast, as seen from the rail of the company ship carrying him to the heart of darkness, is a case in point:

Watching a coast as it slips by the ship is like thinking about an enigma. There it is before you—smiling, frowning, inviting, grand, mean, insipid, or savage, and always mute with an air of whispering, Come and find out. This one was almost featureless, as if still in the making, with an aspect of monotonous grimness. The edge of a colossal jungle, so dark green as to be almost black, fringed with white surf, ran straight, like a ruled line, far, far away along a blue sea whose glitter was blurred by a creeping mist. The sun was fierce, the land seemed to glisten and drip with steam.

(*Heart of Darkness,* p. 13)

Another young captain exercising his first command, this time in *The Shadow-Line,* has his troubles with the island of Koh-ring. In this instance, the captain is trying to put as much distance as possible between his ship and the island, but the sea breeze will not come. The ship is becalmed and the island hovers over the ship as if holding it to the land by some subtle enchantment:

The Island of Koh-ring, a great, black, upheaved ridge amongst a lot of tiny islets, lying upon the glassy water like a triton amongst minnows, seemed to be the center of the fatal circle. It seemed impossible to get away from it. Day after day it remained in sight. More than once, in a favorable breeze, I would take its bearing in the fast ebbing twilight, thinking that it was for the last time. Vain hope. A night of fitful airs would undo the gains of temporary favor, and the rising sun would throw out the black relief of Koh-ring, looking more barren, inhospitable, and grim than ever. (p. 84)

One final example of the land in its ominous and inhospitable

aspect may be cited. There are descriptions of London as seen
from the Thames estuary in *Heart of Darkness* and *The Nigger
of the "Narcissus"* which are remarkably similar in their emphasis
and in their effect. In *Heart of Darkness,* for instance, the narrator, lazing aboard the yawl *Nellie,* glances toward the city, and
through his consciousness we get this picture:

> Only the gloom to the west, brooding over the upper reaches, be-
> came more somber every minute, as if angered by the approach of
> the sun. And at last, in its curved and imperceptible fall, the sun
> sank low, and from glowing white changed to a dull red without rays
> and without heat, as if about to go out suddenly, stricken to death
> by the touch of that gloom brooding over a crowd of men. (p. 4)

It is as if the narrator were describing a sunset over the Congo
and, indeed, Conrad makes the parallel explicit in a passage in
The Mirror of the Sea:

> This stretch of the Thames from London Bridge to the Albert
> Docks is to other watersides of river ports what a virgin forest would
> be to a garden. It is a thing grown up, not made. It recalls a jungle by
> the confused, varied, and impenetrable aspect of the buildings that line
> the shore, not according to a planned purpose, but as if sprung up
> by accident from scattered seeds. Like the matted growth of bushes
> and creepers veiling the silent depths of an unexplored wilderness,
> they hide the depths of London's infinitely varied, vigorous, seeth-
> ing life. (p. 107)

And whatever the appeal of the English Channel, noted earlier in
a passage from *The Nigger of the "Narcissus,"* once the *Narcissus* enters the Thames and moves upriver toward London, the
land presents a very different prospect. It will be observed that
Conrad again stresses the portentous air which surrounds the
city, the dismal gloom, the polluted and teeming atmosphere.
Here, in fact, Conrad resembles nothing so much as a late nine-
teenth-century ecologist:

> The reach narrowed; from both sides the land approached the
> ship. . . . A low cloud hung before her—a great opalescent and tremu-
> lous cloud, that seemed to rise from the steaming brows of millions
> of men. Long drifts of smoky vapors soiled it with livid trails; it
> throbbed to the beat of millions of hearts, and from it came an

immense and lamentable murmur—the murmur of millions of lips praying, cursing, sighing, jeering—the undying murmur of folly, regret, and hope exhaled by the crowds of the anxious earth. The *Narcissus* entered the cloud; the shadows deepened; on all sides there was the clang of iron, the sound of mighty blows, shrieks, yells. . . . A mad jumble of begrimed walls loomed up vaguely in the smoke, bewildering and mournful, like a vision of disaster.

(p. 444)

But the land, in Conrad, is much more than a forbidding but passive presence. There emerges, in fact, from Conrad's pages a well-defined pattern in which the land plays an active role, in which ties with the land or contact with the land can taint, corrupt, degrade, and, finally, destroy both ships and men.

For Conrad and, perhaps, for all seamen who sailed before the mast, the most appealing, the most thoroughly satisfying sight that the eye might behold was a ship at sea, under sail, in fair weather. In an effort to do full justice to this most stirring of spectacles, Conrad invariably describes a sailing ship in terms of a bird in flight. For example, in *The Mirror of the Sea,* in reminiscing about his beloved *Tremolino,* Conrad makes the analogy quite explicit:

In reality, she was a true balancelle, with two short masts raking forward and two curved yards, each as long as her hull; a true child of the Latin Lake, with a spread of two enormous sails resembling the pointed wings on a sea-bird's slender body, and herself, like a bird indeed, skimming rather than sailing the seas. (p. 156)

Consider, however, what happens to a ship, in Conrad, as she nears land, or to a ship in port. The *Narcissus,* it will be recalled from the passage quoted earlier, offers visual delights for the seaman as it enters the Channel, but the ship itself resembles "a great tired bird speeding to its nest" (p. 442). The bird imagery is still here, but it is severely compromised by the qualifying "tired," and something is lost in the substitution of "speeding" for the "skimming . . . the seas" of the *Tremolino* passage. There is a sense of unwarranted haste in "speeding," as if the land exerts some irresistible force on the ship which robs it of its will. And a nesting bird is a rather different thing from a bird in flight.

Later, in *The Mirror of the Sea,* the bird image is given a startling twist. Conrad is describing the dockyards of London:

The view of ships lying moored in some of the older docks of London has always suggested to my mind the image of a flock of swans kept in the flooded backyard of grim tenement houses. (p. 110)

The soaring sea-bird, the free spirit skimming the seas and imbued with grace and beauty, has now been reduced to a flightless creature pent up in landlocked waters, a virtual prisoner of the land. So, too, its squalid place of captivity is in sharp contrast to the splendor of the open sea. The idea of the ship's being captured and held by the land is enlarged upon in a later passage in *The Mirror of the Sea:*

A ship in dock, surrounded by quays and the walls of ware-houses, has the appearance of a prisoner meditating upon freedom in the sadness of a free spirit put under restraint. (p. 115)

It might be noted, in passing, that any close proximity with the land brings about this same reduction in a ship's stature and, more important, in its mobility. In *The Rescue,* for example, Lingard's crew react as follows in seeing the yacht *Hermit* run aground and lying helpless on her side:

There was to the lookers-on aboard the brig something sad and disappointing in the yacht's aspect as she lay perfectly still in an attitude that in a seaman's mind is associated with the idea of rapid motion. (p. 53)

But the loss of its freedom is not the only nor the least injury suffered by a ship in port. It is at the will of land-dwellers, men who are not of the craft and whose unclean and often clumsy hands rob the ship of the last vestige of dignity. In *The Mirror of the Sea*, Conrad speaks with marked exasperation of dock-masters and berthing-masters: "There never seem chains and ropes enough to satisfy their minds concerned with the safe binding of free ships to the strong, muddy, enslaved earth" (p. 115). The captain in "The Secret Sharer" is not only anxious to get the feel of his first command, but also equally anxious to get her out of the hands of shorelings: "Fast alongside a wharf, littered like any ship in port with a tangle of unrelated things, invaded by unrelated shore people, I had hardly seen her yet properly" (p. 652). As soon as the *Narcissus* is safely berthed, we are told that "a swarm of strange men, clambering up her sides, took possession of her in the name of the sordid earth" (p. 446). The key words here are the pejorative "swarm," characterizing the dockyard party, "strange," which suggests that these are callous men who do not know the ship or love the ship as does her crew, and "took possession," echoing once more the note of restriction and captivity.

The *Nan-Shan,* in *Typhoon,* although a steamship and thus a lesser ship in Conrad's mind, undergoes the same indifferent and degrading treatment while in port. This is the scene as the *Nan-Shan* takes on her cargo before the arrival of its unusual consignment of passengers, the Chinese coolies:

> All of them [the winches] were hard at work, snatching slings of cargo, high up, to the end of long derricks, only, as it seemed, to let them rip down recklessly by the run. The cargo chains groaned in the gins, clinked on coamings, rattled over the side; and the whole ship quivered, with her long gray flanks smoking in wreaths of steam. (p. 12)

Throughout these descriptions of the disarray of a ship in port, there is, of course, the implicit contrast with the fixed, deliberate, almost rhythmical order of the ship's routine when at sea. The contrast is enough to incense the naturally methodical and tidy mind of the veteran seaman, and, in the examples given, Conrad's feeling for the fitness of things is obviously outraged.

The land, it might be noted, not only robs ships of their freedom but also actively preys upon its captives. In "Youth," for instance, when the *Judea,* having sprung a critical leak, is forced to put back into Falmouth harbor, Marlow describes the reception accorded the ship thus:

> The good people there live on casualties of the sea, and no doubt were glad to see us. A hungry crowd of shipwrights sharpened their chisels at the sight of that carcass of a ship. And, by Jove! they had pretty pickings off us before they were done. (p. 126)

To further underscore the debilitating effects of the land, there is a marked and revealing contrast in the metaphors which Conrad employs for seagoing ships and for what might be called land ships—tugboats, harbor boats, river steamers. In fact, in establishing his metaphorical terms, Conrad runs the gamut from the soaring, graceful birds of pretty plummage, the terms in which he invariably sees sailing ships, to the lowliest, most ungainly and most unlovely of creatures, the beetle, the image with which Conrad invariably depicts land ships. For example, the tug which takes the *Narcissus* to the outer harbor in Bombay is described as follows:

She resembled an enormous and aquatic blackbeetle, surprised by the light, overwhelmed by the sunshine, trying to escape with ineffectual effort into the distant gloom of the land. She left a lingering smudge of smoke on the sky, and two vanishing trails of foam on the water. On the place where she had stopped a round black patch of soot remained, undulating on the swell—an unclean mark of the creature's rest. (p. 315)

In addition to the central image of the beetle, Conrad's diction, in describing the tug, does much to suggest the soiling and befouling influence of the land on the sea and on the ships which should belong to the sea but are, instead, committed to the land.

The beetle motif appears again in *Heart of Darkness*. Although Marlow comes, in time, to appreciate the "two-penny-half-penny river-steamboat" (p. 12) which he pilots up the Congo, to begin with he is not above the deep-sea sailor's disdain for the essentially land-going craft. As he makes his way through the towering trees which line the river on each side, Marlow describes the progress of his command as "the little begrimed steamboat, like a sluggish beetle crawling on the floor of a lofty portico" (p. 35).

And the metaphor occurs again in *The Rescue,* albeit this time the image, while retaining beetle-like qualities, is drawn from a slightly different branch of the entomological family. Lingard has put out in one of the *Lightning*'s boats seeking a navigable opening to the Shore of Refuge: "Creek after creek was passed and the boat crept on slowly like a monstrous water-spider with a big body and eight slender legs" (p. 94). All of this is reminiscent of Stein's beetles in *Lord Jim* and the association is valid. Just as the beetle metaphor, applied to land ships, implies a close affinity with the land, so too, Stein's collection of beetles, especially as contrasted with the butterflies, suggests his practical, his down-to-earth side. Stein confesses to being a romantic (the butterflies), but, in consulting him about Jim, Marlow makes it clear that Stein is also an eminently realistic and pragmatic man; hence, the beetles.

It is worth observing here that Conrad employs the beetle image in another context in *Lord Jim*, again evoking the most unfavorable of connotations. It will be recalled that the contorted, gliding gait of the abject Cornelius reminds Marlow of nothing so much as "the creeping of a repulsive beetle" (p. 173). So, too, the craven Heemskirk in *Freya of the Seven Isles* is repeatedly compared to a "blackbeetle."

There are other instances in which Conrad draws from the land in order to complete the terms of his metaphors, and, when applied to the sea, the effects are uniformly reductive. Three examples, all taken from "Youth," will perhaps suffice. Of the first, and seemingly successful, attempt to control the fire aboard the *Judea*, Marlow says: "Then the poisonous cloud blew away, and we went back to work in a smoke that was no thicker now than that of an ordinary factory chimney" (p. 131). And, in assaying the effects of the explosion on the *Judea*, Marlow, in evoking the scene of destruction at sea, refers, on two occasions to the land:

> The deck was a wilderness of smashed timber, lying crosswise like trees in a wood after a hurricane. . . . (p. 135)

> The deck was a tangle of planks on edge, of planks on end, of splinters, of ruined woodwork. The masts rose from that chaos like big trees above a matted undergrowth. . . . The smoke of the invisible fire was coming up again, was trailing, like a poisonous thick mist in some valley choked with dead wood. (p. 137)

But, in robbing a ship of its freedom and its vitality, in degrading and despoiling it, the land has not yet done its worst. It is quite capable of committing the ultimate indignity--of taking the ship's life. The fatal effect which the land exerts on ships is hinted at by Conrad on several occasions. For example, in *The Mirror of the Sea*, Conrad sums up his discussion of Departures and Landfalls by observing that with every landfall, the ship is that much nearer extinction. The point is made in a passage which begins with Conrad's remarking that the last command of any voyage is the cry "Let go," the signal to drop anchor:

This is the final word of a ship's ended journey, the closing word
of her toil and of her achievement. In a life whose worth is told
out in passages from port to port, the splash of the anchor's fall
and the thunderous rumbling of the chain are like the closing of a
distant period, of which she seems conscious with a slight deep
shudder of all her frame. By so much is she nearer to her appointed
death, for neither years nor voyages can go on for ever. (p. 22)

To be fair and not to misconstrue, it must be pointed out that
here Conrad is chiefly concerned with the life expectancy, the
mere physical durability of the ship. Here, the land is again a
passive agent—the landfall serving as a measure of the life cycle
of the ship, just as the passing year is an index in the life cycle
of man.

The land does, however, possess the power to destroy and
to do so actively. The land as a destructive force, bringing about
the death of a ship, is best seen in the closing passages of *The
Nigger of the "Narcissus."* As the *Narcissus* passes the Downs,
in the Channel, the speed of the "great tired bird" is markedly
reduced, and on entering the reaches of the Thames, the ship
becomes a captive bird. The proud spirit, once free for flight
about the world, is taken in tow, and, "Shorn of the glory of her
white wings," Conrad says, "she wound obediently after the tug
through the maze of invisible channels" (p. 443). The *Narcissus*
is already a sadly diminished thing, but the reductive power of
the land has only begun to operate.

This reduction is brought about by a process of constriction.
The ship is first robbed of her freedom of flight and then, gradu-
ally, her freedom of any movement is restricted. This constricting and restricting effect may be noted in the following passages:

The reach narrowed; from both sides the land approached the ship
. . . the land, closing in, stepped between the ship and the sea.
(p. 444)

The stony shores ran away right and left in straight lines, enclosing
a somber and rectangular pool. Brick walls rose high above the
water—soulless walls, staring through hundreds of windows as
troubled and dull as the eyes of overfed brutes. At their base monstrous iron cranes crouched, with chains hanging from their long
necks, balancing cruel-looking hooks over the decks of lifeless
ships. (p. 445)

(There may be some irony in the fact that an artificial bird, the crane, awkward as the creature for which it is named, dominates the once sleek and agile flying birds of the sea.) The chief thrust of the passage, however, is the strong suggestion that the *Narcissus,* now inert and powerless to help herself, is being maneuvered into a graveyard of ships. And, as she docks, the land applies the last bit of pressure, which proves mortal for the ship:

The *Narcissus* came gently into her berth; the shadows of soulless walls fell upon her, the dust of all the continents leaped upon her deck, and a swarm of strange men, clambering up her sides, took possession of her in the name of the sordid earth. She had ceased to live. (p. 446)

(We can forgive, I submit, Conrad's apparent obsession with "soulless walls," since the effectiveness of the image justifies the repetition.) The passage is otherwise quite explicit; the *Narcissus,* funereal ashes having been scattered upon her (somewhat hastily and indecently), is dead and it is the land which has brought about her end. The death of the ship is, of course, figurativ=, since the *Narcissus* will sail again. And yet, there is a sense in which it may be said that the end of a voyage marks the death of a ship. A ship is truly alive only at sea and any ship standing motionless and powerless and purposeless in dock has, indeed, "ceased to live."

As it is with ships, so it is with men. The potential of the land to taint, to corrupt, and, finally, to kill, can be seen again in observing what happens to so many of Conrad's seamen who are too long on land or who preserve too close ties with the land.

On the lowest and least harmful level, there are extraordinary mutations which take place among seamen exposed to prolonged contact with the land. For example, ashore and without a ship, the highly competent, urbane, and tactful Charlie Marlow becomes, to speak bluntly, a pain in the neck. In *Heart of Darkness,* Marlow speaks of just such an extended period on the beach:

I had then, as you remember, just returned to London after a lot of Indian Ocean, Pacific, China Seas—a regular dose of the East— six years or so, and I was loafing about, hindering you fellows in your work and invading your homes, just as though I had got a heavenly mission to civilize you. (pp. 7–8)

The redeeming element, of course, is the fact that Marlow is
to recognize his shortcomings and to speak of them lightly.
the playfulness is gone, later, when Marlow's involuntary
action forces him to compromise his principles and turn to a
woman for help, to the "dear enthusiastic soul," his aunt, who
nearly drives Marlow over the edge with her pious mouthings
about the virtues of the Belgian trading company he is about to
join. In a sense, it is Marlow's inability to get back to the safety
of the sea, or, to put it another way, the unavoidably protracted
stay ashore, which brings him to the heart of darkness.

This motif of the fish out of water, the seaman ashore, is
echoed at several points in Conrad. For instance, the unnamed
narrator in *The Shadow-Line,* having given up his ship, recognizes that his status has changed and he recognizes the fact in a
rather peculiar way:

Being now a man without a ship, and having for a time broken my
connection with the sea—become, in fact, a mere potential passenger—it would have been more appropriate perhaps if I had gone
to stay at an hotel. There it was, too, within a stone's throw of the
Harbor Office, low, but somehow palatial, displaying its white,
pillared pavilions surrounded by trim grass plots. I would have felt
a passenger indeed in there! I gave it a hostile glance and directed
my steps towards the Officers' Sailors' Home. (p. 8)

Fortunately for the narrator, his stay on land is brief, so brief,
in fact, that when the opportunity comes to take over the vacant
command in Bangkok, both Captain Giles and Captain Ellis
consider him the only man in port fit for the job. The basis of
their joint reasoning is that the narrator has not been ashore
long enough to be captivated or corrupted. Jim, it will be remembered, is not so lucky. His stay in the hospital in Singapore
is of some duration and the demoralizing influence of other seamen who have been too long ashore is manifest in the following:

The majority were men who, like himself, thrown there by some
accident, had remained as officers of country ships. They had now
a horror of the home service, with its harder conditions, severer
view of duty, and the hazard of stormy oceans. They were attuned
to the eternal peace of Eastern sky and sea . . . in all they said—
in their actions, in their looks, in their persons—could be detected

the soft spot, the place of decay, the determination to lounge safely through existence. (*Lord Jim,* p. 9)

As a result, when he is fit again Jim turns his back on the home service and signs on as mate of the ill-favored and ill-fated *Patna.*

Conrad himself confessed to feeling the enervating effects of a long stay ashore. In *A Personal Record,* he described the period of idleness, just before he set to work in earnest on *Almayer's Folly,* in these terms:

My whole being was steeped deep in the indolence of a sailor away from the sea, the scene of never-ending labor and of unceasing duty. For utter surrender to indolence you cannot beat a sailor ashore when that mood is on him—the mood of absolute irresponsibility tasted to the full. (pp. 73–74)

Then there is the case, in *Lord Jim,* of Little Bob Stanton, the hero of the *Sephora* disaster. Marlow attributes Stanton's leaving the sea, his "spell of shore-life," as Marlow calls it (p. 92) to a misguided love affair. Stanton, according to Marlow, "fondly hoped he had done with the sea for ever, and made sure he had got hold of all the bliss on earth" (p. 92), but the prospective idyllic existence ashore also involves a humdrum job as an insurance salesman; " . . . my immortal soul," Stanton is quoted as saying, "was shrivelled down to the size of a parched pea after a week of that work" (p. 92). Stanton returns to the sea and later perishes, with the *Sephora,* in a valiant effort to save the life of a panic-stricken passenger.

The most striking example, in Conrad, of the debilitating effects of the land is the Jekyll-Hyde transformation which takes place in old Singleton, the indomitable helmsman of the *Narcissus.* Aboard ship, Singleton (as his name suggests) is peerless Conrad's master mold of the dedicated seaman; ashore, he becomes a drunken lout who is pathetically out of his element It is Singleton's boast that of the very few days he has been ashore during the past forty-five years, on even fewer days ha he been "in a condition to distinguish daylight" (p. 296). Even more telling of Singleton's reduced stature when ashore is the scene in the Board of Trade Office as the *Narcissus*'s crew are paid off. Singleton, whose hands were responsive to the slightes

nuance of the ship's movements during his thirty-hour vigil at
the wheel, makes an awkward "heavy cross" in signing the pay-
roll and clumsily blots the page while doing so. He disappears
from the story at this point and is dismissed by one of the Board
of Trade "birds" as a "disgusting old brute" (p. 449).

And the land has its effect on others of the *Narcissus*'s complement. The worthy Captain Allistoun, whom Donkin could
single out as a target for his belaying pin on the darkest night at
sea, goes ashore with his wife, unrecognized. So, too, the status
of the crew has changed markedly; assigned to regular watches
and specific duties aboard ship and made to account for every
minute of their time, the crew, wandering about Tower Hill
after being dismissed, are seen by the narrator as "castaways,"
that is, men deposited without warning on an alien shore. Only
the unspeakable Donkin, who is a kind of nautical mistake anyway, is at home and at ease on land.

The capacity of the land to taint, to debase and to degrade
is perhaps best summed up by Mr. B——, in Conrad's mind the
best chief mate afloat. On one of the numerous occasions in *The
Mirror of the Sea* when Conrad guides the mate to his cabin at
night, Mr. B—— offers this bit of inebriated wisdom: "Ports are
no good—ships rot, men go to the devil! . . . I wish she were at
sea out of this" (p. 127).

But, if the mere association with the land can be reductive
for the seaman, the preservation of or the cultivating of ties
ashore can be ruinous. The single weakness, in this context, in
the otherwise admirable Captain Beard, of "Youth," is his wholly
natural fondness for his amiable wife. This fondness, however
natural and understandable it may be, does not constitute a
dispensation for Beard's violating a cardinal rule of the sea and
of command. He has his wife aboard while his ship is loading in
Newcastle harbor. When the *Judea* is nearly rammed by the
errant steamer, Beard finds his commitment to his ship seriously
compromised. And he finds himself adrift in the ship's boat where
he had retreated with his wife in the moment of danger. The
insidious influence of the land is clearly exemplified in this episode.
Not only has Beard been remiss in his duty to the ship, but also
such was his haste to put his wife out of peril that he had set out

without oars and was now drifting aimlessly about the dock. The youthful Marlow is overwhelmed by this exhibition of devotion: "Just imagine that old fellow saving heroically in his arms that old woman—the woman of his life" (p. 121). Beard, however, puts the incident in its proper perspective (proper, that is, for the captain of the *Judea,* albeit not for Mrs. Beard's husband) with his rueful comment: "A sailor has no business with a wife— I say. There I was, out of the ship" (p. 121). Beard's final word on the episode is evidence both of the fact that he has recovered and is again master of the *Judea* and of his awareness of his luck in that he and the ship escaped unscathed: "Well, no harm done this time. Let's go and look at what that fool of a steamer smashed" (p. 121).

Captain Whalley of the steamship *Sofala,* in *The End of the Tether,* is not so lucky. The tie which binds him to the land takes its full toll. In order to recoup his losses by collecting on the ship's insurance, Massy, the engineer and chief owner of the *Sofala,* deliberately disorients the compass by placing his coat, its pockets filled with pieces of iron, near it. As a result, the *Sofala* smashes itself against the reefs. On discovering Massy's perfidy, Captain Whalley's initial reaction is that of the honorable man and the outraged seaman: "He made me lose a ship" (p. 605). Whalley prepares to abandon ship, taking the incriminating evidence of the coat with him to be presented to the Board of Inquiry. On reflection, however, he realizes that if it is established that the ship was sunk deliberately, there will be no compensation from the insurance company. His widowed daughter, Ivy, in Melbourne, whom he largely supports and for whom he has borne the indignity of piloting the ancient *Sofala,* will not be repaid the £500 which Whalley has invested in the ship. Faced with this unacceptable prospect, Whalley places the iron in his own pockets to insure that he will not attempt to save himself and goes down with the ship. Whalley has not only compromised his honor, he is also an accessory, although admittedly after the fact, in what Marlow in *Heart of Darkness* (p. 35) calls "the unpardonable sin" for a seaman; he has failed to keep his ship afloat. The dereliction is the more heinous in that Whalley has knowingly, and thus willingly, conspired in the loss of a ship. And all for the love of Ivy.

The two chief exhibits in Conrad's case against maintaining or initiating ties ashore, the two Conradian seamen most deeply involved with the land, are Jim and Tom Lingard. An extended discussion of these two misdirected seamen falls, more properly, into a later chapter. It is perhaps sufficient to suggest here that both men would have done well to remain at sea. Both err in turning to the land. Jim, a failure at sea, attempts to redeem his failure on the land; Lingard, an eminent success at sea, attempts to extend his success to the land. Both attempts are not only disastrous for themselves, but also, tragically, for others for whom the two have accepted a measure of responsibility, in some instances the full measure.

The analogy of the vulnerability of ships to that of men set up earlier prevails to the ultimate degree. Not only does the land taint, corrupt, and degrade men, as it does ships, but also its proximity can be just as fatal for men as it is for ships.

The young captain of *The Shadow-Line,* for instance, finds that his first command is a pest ship. He is convinced that the fever which threatens to decimate his crew and turn his ship into a lifeless derelict is a macabre heritage from the land. He is equally convinced that, not satisfied with having implanted the contagion aboard his ship, the land now holds the ship in thrall and will not release it until all life aboard is destroyed. How else to explain the dead calm, the failure of the sea breeze that would end the spell and take the ship to the pure air of the open sea? The active malevolence of the land clearly emerges in the following passage, the captain's anguished appraisal of his situation:

. . . if we had only had a little more wind, only a very little more, we might, we should, have been abreast of Liant by this time and increasing our distance from that contaminated shore. And it was not only the distance. It seemed to me that a stronger breeze would have blown away the infection which clung to the ship. It obviously did cling to the ship. Two men. One burning, one shivering. I felt a distinct reluctance to go and look at them. What was the good? Poison is poison. Tropical fever is tropical fever. But that it should have stretched its claw after us over the sea seemed to me an extraordinary and unfair license. (p. 79)

The captain and his ship ultimately escape, the land having presented to them only the threat of death.

Jimmy Wait, in *The Nigger of the "Narcissus,"* however, does not escape and it is in this novel that the most clear-cut evidence of the deadly nature, for man, of the proximity of the land is to be found. By all standards, Jimmy is a long time dying, so much so that the crew, having once rescued him from death, are now virtually convinced that by a combined effort of the will, by willing him not to die, they can save Jimmy Wait again. In so doing, they will cheat death not only for Jimmy's sake, but also for their own sake. The crew's reasoning might be put forth in an inversion of Donne's pronouncement; if the bell does not toll for Jimmy Wait, it will toll for no man.

In this splendid illusion, the crew are overlooking the decree of old Singleton, that Jimmy's time is not yet. Rather, he will die "in sight of land. Always so," Singleton declares (p. 412). Elsewhere (p. 423) Singleton assures the crew that "Jimmy knew that the land would draw his life from him." On the practical level, of course, Singleton's verdict emerges as a kind of nautical old wives' tale. Yet, in the novel, Singleton enjoys infallibility on matters concerning the sea and his judgments thereon are not to be questioned. It is significant that the narrator does not attempt to gainsay him, and, indeed, it is just as well that he does not make the attempt. On the appointed day, as the ship sails by the Azores, Jimmy Wait expires. Within sight of the land that takes life away, Jimmy "had ceased to breathe" (p. 435).

With the death of Jimmy Wait, we arrive at a conjunction of two central ideas which have been examined at some length in this chapter—the capacity, even the avidity, of the land to destroy ships and its equally virulent power to destroy men. This conjunction is best effected in *The Nigger of the "Narcissus"* and it is most visible in the striking similarities to be found in Conrad's handling of the two deaths around which the novel is structured, the figurative death of the *Narcissus* and the very literal death of its Nigger.

It will be recalled that as the ship makes its way up the English Channel, it becomes noticeably reduced in stature. Earlier, Conrad (or his narrator, if you will) has described the

Narcissus at sea as "a high and lonely pyramid, gliding, all shining and white, through the sunlit mist" (p. 315). On entering the Channel, however, she is diminished to the "great tired bird speeding to its nest" (p. 442). And the reductive process has only just begun. She is soon "shorn of the glory of her white wings" (p. 443) and robbed of the power of flight. Unable now to proceed under her own power, she follows the beetle-like tug "obediently." As the *Narcissus* berths, she is so weakened and diminished that a few men "with checkropes" are able to handle her with ease. The ship which, at sea, supported and controlled the destinies of the many men on her decks, is now mastered and maneuvered about by a mere handful of men. Finally, the *Narcissus* lies in dock, inert, immobile, lifeless.

That it is the presence of the land which has wrought this extraordinary transformation is made quite clear. Conrad takes pains, in fact, to direct the reader's attention to the role which the land plays in the *Narcissus*'s demise. We are told that "from both sides the land approached the ship" (p. 444) and, later, that "the land, closing in, stepped between the ship and the sea" (p. 444). What is taking place is a form of restriction or constriction; the land limits the ship's range of movement more and more: "She moved through a narrow lane of water between two low walls of granite . . . the stony shores ran away right and left in straight lines, enclosing a somber and rectangular pool" (p. 445). The ship's berth, significantly, is a "pool," a place of dead water, and, in its rectangularity, it takes on the appearance of a grave. Ultimately, the contracting and constricting force of the land is such that the very life is squeezed out of the ship: "She had ceased to live" (p. 446).

Similarly, at the outset of the tale, Jimmy Wait is an imposing figure. We are told he "overtopped the tallest by half a head" (p. 306), and as Jimmy boards ship his booming voice dominates the deck. So imposing, in fact, is Jimmy Wait that the chief mate, Mr. Baker, who judges Jimmy a "fine, big man that" (p. 308), and Creighton, the second officer, engage in a mild rivalry for his services in their respective watches. But, the reductive process observed in connection with the ship can be seen again in Jimmy's case. Very soon, he is reduced from the "fine, big man" of Baker's miscalculation to an invalid who is obliged to "lay up" in the *Narcissus*'s makeshift sick bay. When Jimmy's shipmates pull him out of the deckhouse during the storm, they are shocked to find him "only a cold black skin loosely stuffed with soft cotton wool" (p. 356). As the ship nears land, Jimmy's diminution becomes more pronounced; his breathing is that "of a man with a hundred-weight or so on the breastbone" (p. 393) and he is "no heavier than an empty beef cask" (p. 413). When he tries to stand, he reels about and can move only when supported on both sides and guided in his steps.

It is scarcely to be overlooked that the constrictive effects of the consumption which ravages Jimmy are of a pattern with the land's becoming ever narrower and confining the ship's capacity for movement, taking its strength and, so to speak, robbing it of the breath of life, the sea breeze. For, in fulfillment of Singleton's prophecy, the land closes in on Jimmy Wait, too, diminishes him, weakens him, and finally squeezes the breath of life from him; "he had ceased to breathe" (p. 435). (In this context, while it may be only an extraordinary coincidence in phrasing, one cannot help but be struck by the remarkable similarity of the diction Conrad employs in describing the death of the ship, "she had ceased to live," and the death of Jimmy Wait, "he had ceased to breathe." Conscious or not on Conrad's part, the parallel is there and it brings the two deaths into even closer proximity.)

In sum, Singleton's somewhat imaginative postulate turns out to be very close to the fact; the land does, indeed, draw life away, from ships and men alike, and in substantially the same way.

It is apparent that Tom Lingard's observation with which this chapter began needs emending, by enlargement. It would be more accurate to say that the only place for an honest man, or for a stout ship, is the sea. It is true that, on occasion, the land may deign to permit the seaman a favorable landfall and, on occasion, it may offer him an attractive vista. More often, however, the land is alien to both ships and men. Ideally, it is to be shunned; at best, it is to be approached warily; above all, it is not to be trusted.

CHAPTER TWO

THE SEA

I had nearly fought my way out. Out to the sea. The sea which was pure, safe, and friendly. —*The Shadow-Line*

He . . . who, putting his trust in the friendship of the sea, neglects the strength and cunning of his right hand, is a fool!
—*The Mirror of the Sea*

The most amazing wonder of the deep is its unfathomable cruelty. —*The Mirror of the Sea*

If we accept Tom Lingard's judgment on the relationship of the seaman and the sea, then the last word has been spoken. For, it will be recalled, Lingard has not said that the sea is the *best* place for the seaman; he has said it is the *only* place. In Lingard's view, the sea is the seaman's natural environment and his spiritual home. He belongs there.

And, if we turn elsewhere in Conrad, the validity of Lingard's assessment seems to gain support. Mr. B—, the best of all chief mates, in *The Mirror of the Sea,* certainly concurs. There is blunt, seamanlike conviction in his "I wish she were at sea out of this," born of his vexation at seeing his ship delayed in port and his disgust at the role of Jack Tar Ashore to which his idleness has driven him. The captain in *The Shadow-Line* would certainly agree with Lingard. It is he who utters the line about the "pure, safe, and friendly" sea which is used as an epigraph to this chapter. He has centered all his hopes of survival on getting his ship to sea. To the doctor who treats his fever-stricken crew, before leaving Bangkok, he remarks anxiously, "I suppose the only thing now is to take care of them

29

as you are doing, till I can get the ship to sea?" (p. 67), and the
captain's faith in the efficacy of the sea is evident when he
sums up the fever which has crippled his ship as "the last desperate pluck of the evil from which we were escaping into the
clean breath of the sea" (p. 79). The young captain in "The
Secret Sharer," savoring the felicity of his first command, would
almost certainly subscribe to Lingard's conviction. As he surveys
the peaceful harbor about him from the rail of his own ship, he
enjoys a moment of total gratification in his membership in the
craft:

. . . I rejoiced in the great security of the sea as compared with the
unrest of the land, in my choice of that untempted life presenting
no disquieting problems, invested with an elementary moral beauty
by the absolute straightforwardness of its appeal and by the singleness of its purpose. (p. 653)

There is a touch of irony in the captain's satisfaction, since the
imminent advent of Leggatt will present him with the most
disquieting of problems. However, the irony is irony of situation;
the captain is not aware of his impending trial and the sincerity
of his words is in no way compromised.

On several occasions, Charlie Marlow seems to be saying
"Amen" to Lingard's pronouncement on the seaman and the
sea; and we can usually trust Marlow, except, perhaps, when
he is pontificating or playing the inscrutable Buddha. (On these
occasions, it should be noted, the reader is invariably properly
oriented by the interplay of irony between Conrad and the reader
from which Marlow is excluded.) There is, then, no reason to
question the sincerity or the enthusiasm of the rhetorical question Marlow directs to his audience, seamen all, at the end of
"Youth," a question which, while centering on youth as the
ideal time, also points to the sea as the ideal place:

. . . tell me, wasn't that the best time, that time when we were young
at sea; young and had nothing, on the sea that gives nothing, except
hard knocks—and sometimes a chance to feel your strength—that
only—that you all regret? (p. 154)

Or, consider Marlow in _Heart of Darkness._ In the midst of the
lunatic world in which he finds himself as he skirts the African

continent, Marlow, the seaman, turns to the sea, something he understands and recognizes, not so much for comfort as, almost, to preserve his sanity: "The voice of the surf heard now and then was a positive pleasure, like the speech of a brother. It was something natural, that had its reason, that had a meaning" (p. 13). And, in *Lord Jim,* Marlow's first sight of the "impeccable world," the sea, after a month in Patusan, is charged with feeling:

The boat fairly flew; we sweltered side by side in the stagnant, superheated air; the smell of mud, of marsh, the primeval smell of fecund earth, seemed to sting our faces; till suddenly at a bend it was as if a great hand far away had lifted a heavy curtain, had flung open an immense portal. The light itself seemed to stir, the sky above our heads widened, a far-off murmur reached our ears, a freshness enveloped us, filled our lungs, quickened our thoughts, our blood, our regrets—and, straight ahead, the forests sank down against the dark blue ridge of the sea.

I breathed deeply, I revelled in the vastness of the opened horizon, in the different atmosphere that seemed to vibrate with a toil of life, with the energy of an impeccable world. This sky and this sea were open to me . . . there was a sign, a call in them—something to which I responded with every fibre of my being. (p. 201)

There are other instances where Conrad is not content merely to join Lingard in pleading the cause of the sea in somewhat general terms. Instead, he demonstrates, explicitly, the salutary effect of the sea and defines the many facets of the sea's appeal. A ship prepared to go to sea, for example, is a vastly different entity from a ship in port preparing to go to sea. In contrast to the disarray that prevails aboard a ship in dock, her decks cluttered with the unfamiliar implements of shipwrights and cargo handlers, a ship on weighing anchor is a model of order, tidiness, and precision. In a word, she is "shipshape," as is the *Narcissus* on the eve of her departure from Bombay:

The ship was ready for sea. The carpenter had driven in the last wedge of the main-hatch battens, and, throwing down his maul, had wiped his face with great deliberation, just on the stroke of five. The decks had been swept, the windlass oiled and made ready to heave up the anchor; the big towrope lay in long bights along one side of the main deck, with one end carried up and hung over the bows, in readiness for the tug . . . (pp. 292–93)

In the same vein, Conrad writes glowingly, in *The Mirror of the Sea,* of the benign nature of the seaman's regimen:

It is a great doctor for sore hearts and sore heads, too, your ship's routine, which I have seen soothe—at least for a time—the most turbulent of spirits. There is health in it, and peace, and satisfaction of the accomplished round; for each day of the ship's life seems to close a circle within the wide ring of the sea horizon. It borrows a certain dignity of sameness from the majestic monotony of the sea. He who loves the sea loves also the ship's routine. (p. 7)

The contrast between the many demands of the ship's routine, which, when met, result in the seaman's well-being, and the aimless and indolent existence which the sailor follows while ashore should not be overlooked. With this passage we encounter a central theme in Conrad, a theme which will be considered at length in a later chapter, namely, the therapeutic and redeeming nature of work. The theme is recurrent in Conrad. It occurs, for instance, in a passage from *The Nigger of the "Narcissus"* which bespeaks both the value of work and the special grace of life at sea:

The men working about the deck were healthy and contented—as most seamen are, when once well out to sea. The true peace of God begins at any spot a thousand miles from the nearest land; and when He sends there the messengers of His might it is not in terrible wrath against crime, presumption, and folly, but paternally, to chasten simple hearts—ignorant hearts that know nothing of life, and beat undisturbed by envy or greed. (p. 319)

In cataloguing the many ways in which the sea makes its appeal, Conrad does not overlook the romance and the mystery which, over the centuries, have prompted so many men to try their skill, and their luck, on the sea. For example, there is romance in full measure in Marlow's evocation, in "Youth," of his first landfall on a Far Eastern coast. The situation, in fact, fairly begs for romantic treatment—the twenty-year-old seaman sailing as second mate for the first time, surviving the fire at sea, and bringing his "first command," the cockleshell of the

Judea safely to shore—and Marlow makes the most of the opportunity:

And this is how I see the East. I have seen its secret places and have looked into its very soul; but now I see it always from a small boat, a high outline of mountains, blue and afar in the morning; like faint mist at noon; a jagged wall of purple at sunset. I have the feel of the oar in my hand, the vision of a scorching blue sea in my eyes. And I see a bay, a wide bay, smooth as glass and polished like ice, shimmering in the dark. A red light burns far off upon the gloom of the land, and the night is soft and warm. We drag at the oars with aching arms, and suddenly a puff of wind, a puff faint and tepid and laden with strange odors of blossoms, of aromatic wood, comes out of the still night—the first sigh of the East on my face. (pp. 148–49)

And, in propria persona, Conrad touches the note of romance again, in *The Mirror of the Sea,* when he conjures up his early recollections of the Mediterranean, the sea which Conrad calls, in a phrase itself properly romantic, "the Nursery of the Craft," and on which he began his career as a seaman:

Happy he who, like Ulysses, has made an adventurous voyage; and there is no such sea for adventurous voyages as the Mediterranean—the inland sea which the ancients looked upon as so vast and so full of wonders. . . . The charm of the Mediterranean dwells in the unforgettable flavor of my early days, and to this hour this sea, upon which the Romans alone ruled without dispute, has kept for me the fascination of youthful romance. (pp. 151–52)

And yet, though Conrad does occasionally extol the virtues of the sea—the order and method of the ship's routine, the salubrious nature of the seaman's way of life, the glamor and romance of the sea itself — it would be hasty to assume that Conrad accepts, without reservation, Lingard's uncomplicated enthusiasm for the sea. A good deal more needs to be said and a number of qualifications need to be made.

For instance, Conrad has no illusions about the sea. Conrad's reader will have to search his pages with great care in order to find the sea with which the reader is most familiar, the sparkling and serene sea of the travel brochure, the sea of the poet and the painter, the sea, in other words, idealized and as seen by the land dweller viewing it from shore. I can offer but two instances of a totally benign sea in Conrad. One instance occurs in 'The Nigger of the "Narcissus." After the gale has passed, the Narcissus, righted again, under sail once more and headed into the wind, luxuriates in the sunshine of the South Atlantic:

In the morning the ship, beginning another day of her wandering life, had an aspect of sumptuous freshness, like the springtime of the earth. The washed decks glistened in a long clear stretch; the oblique sunlight struck the yellow brasses in dazzling splashes, darted over the polished rods in lines of gold, and the single drops of salt water forgotten here and there along the rail were as limpid as drops of dew, and sparkled more than scattered diamonds. The sails slept, hushed by a gentle breeze. The sun, rising lonely and splendid in the blue sky, saw a solitary ship gliding close-hauled on the blue sea. (p. 414)

A second instance of a placid sea in Conrad occurs in "Youth." There is a brief lull in the progress of the fire which has broken out in the Judea's hold and Conrad describes this interlude of calm as follows:

The sky was a miracle of purity, a miracle of azure. The sea was polished, was blue, was pellucid, was sparkling like a precious stone, extending on all sides, all round to the horizon — as if the whole terrestrial globe had been one jewel, one colossal sapphire, a single gem fashioned into a planet. (p. 132)

At first reading Conrad's well-known description, in Lord Jim, of the Patna crossing the Arabian Gulf in the darkness would appear to be in the same vein, a passage depicting an ocean at peace, a night scene creating an ambience of harmony, serenity, and security:

A marvelous stillness pervaded the world, and the stars, together with the serenity of their rays, seemed to shed upon the earth the assurance of everlasting security. The young moon recurved, and, shining low in the west, was like a slender shaving thrown up from a bar of gold, and the Arabian Sea, smooth and cool to the eye like a sheet of ice, extended its perfect level to the perfect circle of a dark horizon. The propeller turned without a check, as though its beat had been part of the scheme of a safe universe; and on each side of the Patna two deep folds of water, permanent and somber on the unwrinkled shimmer, enclosed within their straight and diverging ridges a few white swirls of foam bursting in a low hiss, a few wavelets, a few ripples, a few undulations that, left behind, agitated the surface of the sea for an instant after the passage of the ship, subsided splashing gently, calmed down at last into the circular stillness of water and sky with the black speck of the moving hull remaining everlastingly in its center. (p. 11)

The surface atmosphere of this passage is one of peace, of placidity, and, to use a key term which Conrad employs very early in the passage, of security. But, a thoughtful and analytical reading yields a number of disturbing undertones. Admittedly, there is a danger here of "reading in," since, on a second reading, we are aware of what is about to befall the *Patna*. However, "the game is worth the candle"; the threatening note underlying the passage, while muted, *is* there. The passage deceives, and in so doing, it is a skillful verbal analogue of the way in which the peaceful night scene at sea deceives Jim. Note, for instance, how Conrad overstates the case; while such overstatement is an unwitting failing on Conrad's part in some instances, here the exaggeration is deliberate. It is, we are advised, a "marvellous" stillness which pervades the scene, and it leads to a sense of "everlasting" security. The virtually motionless sea extends its "perfect" level to the "perfect" circle of the horizon. Conrad surely doth protest too much. It is all too perfect. The steady revolutions of the propeller are likened to a heartbeat; a conventional enough metaphor, but Conrad overlooks (or does he?) that the heart is a highly unpredictable organ. Equally conventional is the propensity of the heart to skip a beat, or to stand still. But, suggestive as this metaphor is, it remains, in the last analysis, speculative. What is quite explicit in this passage, however, is the unremitting insistence on the theme of security. The sea, the ship, and the sky are part of a scheme of a "safe" universe; the wake of the *Patna* is a "permanent" phenomenon; the slight agitation caused by the ship's passing, an intrusion on the placidity of the scene, lasts only an "instant." The *Patna* steams on, at the close of the passage, a black speck "everlastingly" in the center of a circular "stillness," and the passage has come full circle from stillness to stillness, with nothing in between to disturb the ship's uneventful progress. It is simply too much, and it creates some misgivings in the reader's mind. Then there is the further hint, in some of the diction which Conrad

employs, that all is not entirely well. The wake of the *Patna,* for
instance, produces a "low hiss" and it disappears in "undulations" behind the ship. (Later, it will be recalled, Jim will ob-
serve that the *Patna* went over "whatever it was as easy as a
snake crawling over a stick" [p. 17].) Similarly, in the final line
of the passage, Conrad speaks of the *Patna* as a "hull," a
curious term for a seaman to use in reference to a ship, unless
he would conjure up visions of an empty and derelict ship or
would foreshadow the damaged bulkhead which Jim mistakenly
concludes to be fatal for the ship.

What ultimately emerges from this passage is a view of the
sea which is not evident from land but one with which the seaman is quite familiar and with which he must, at some time,
come to terms. This is a deceitful, cunning, and fraudulent sea,
a sea without a conscience, a sea which lulls the careless seaman
into a false sense of security, a sea whose chief wonder is, as
Conrad so knowingly puts it, "its unfathomable cruelty."

Jim protests, on several occasions when speaking of the
Patna incident, that he was taken unaware and treated unfairly
by the sea. But Conrad, or Marlow, or any experienced seaman,
while making some allowance for Jim's youth, would dismiss his
protestations by saying that he should have known better. Later
in *Lord Jim,* Marlow, in the midst of one of his soaring flights
of rhetoric, observes that, for the young seaman, the face of the
sea is veiled indeed and that, at the outset of his career, he will
mistake the appearance of the sea's benevolence for the reality:
"In no other kind of life is the illusion more wide of reality—in
no other is the beginning *all* illusion" (p. 79). Characteristically,
Marlow fails to define the precise nature of this illusion, but it
is reasonable to assume that he has in mind such illusory sentiments as are to be found in the following passage from *The Mirror of the Sea,* a passage representing, it seems to me, either a
lapse of memory or a moment of charity on Conrad's part:

Water is friendly to man. The ocean, a part of Nature farthest
removed in the unchangeableness and majesty of its might from
the spirit of mankind, has ever been a friend to the enterprising
nations of the earth. And of all the elements this is the one to which
men have always been prone to trust themselves, as if its immensity

held a reward as vast as itself. (p. 101)

This, I propose, is the illusion, and this passage is a marked exception to Conrad's usual attitude toward the sea. Virtually everywhere else in the two memoirs and in the sea stories, the notion of a benign sea is treated as the dangerous and destructive fraud that it is.

The saving grace is that the illusion doesn't last forever. In the passage quoted above on the sea's ability to create the illusion of benevolence, Marlow goes on to say that, fortunately, the disenchantment is swift. Marlow is, however, mistaken. The disenchantment is *sure,* if one remains at sea long enough, but it may not come until rather late in the game. Old Singleton, for example, spends nearly all of his life at sea before he becomes fully aware of the sea's capacity to play the cheat:

He looked upon the immortal sea with the awakened and groping perception of its heartless might; he saw it unchanged, black and foaming under the eternal scrutiny of the stars; he heard its impatient voice calling for him out of a pitiless vastness full of unrest, of turmoil, and of terror. He looked afar upon it, and he saw an immensity tormented and blind, moaning and furious, that claimed all the days of his tenacious life, and, when life was over, would claim the worn-out body of its slave.

(*The Nigger of the "Narcissus,"* p. 382)

Captain MacWhirr, in *Typhoon,* has also been deceived over the years. We are told that he had "wandered innocently over the waters with the only visible purpose of getting food, raiment, and house-room for three people ashore" (p. 18); and his enlightenment, modest though it is, does not come until late in his career. MacWhirr has been at sea since the age of fifteen, but it is not until the advent of the hurricane that he is given "a glimpse of immeasurable strength and of immoderate wrath, the wrath that passes exhausted but never appeased—the wrath and fury of the passionate sea" (pp. 18–19).

And even the King of the Sea, Tom Lingard, dedicated though he is to the virtues of the sea and the seaman's way of life, arrives at a moment of disenchantment. In *The Rescue,* just as he is ready to carry out his grand design of returning Hassim to power, Lingard finds that the sea has played him false. It has intervened in his plans by presenting him with the unexpected and vexing problem of the stranded yacht:

Lingard, unconscious of everything and everybody, contemplated the sea. He had grown on it, he had lived with it; it had enticed him away from home; on it his thoughts had expanded and his hand had found work to do. It had suggested endeavor, it had made him owner and commander of the finest brig afloat; it had lulled him into a belief in himself, in his strength, in his luck—and suddenly, by its complicity in a fatal accident, it had brought him face to face with a difficulty that looked like the beginning of disaster.
(p. 127)

The awakening to the sea's ability to cheat and defraud, the awareness of the extent of the sea's perfidy comes to all seamen eventually, not only in the pages of fiction but also in real life. Conrad is merely echoing the combined wisdom of a number of his seafarers in the following confession, from *The Mirror of the Sea,* of his own disenchantment:

Already I looked with other eyes upon the sea. I knew it capable of betraying the generous ardor of youth as implacably as, indifferent to evil and good, it would have betrayed the basest greed or the noblest heroism. My conception of its magnanimous greatness was gone. And I looked upon the true sea—the sea that plays with men till their hearts are broken, and wears stout ships to death. Nothing can touch the brooding bitterness of its soul. Open to all and faithful to none, it exercises its fascination for the undoing of the best. To love it is not well. It knows no bond of plighted troth, no fidelity to misfortune, to long companionship, to long devotion. The promise it holds out perpetually is very great; but the only secret of its possession is strength, strength—the jealous, sleepless strength of a man guarding a coveted treasure within his gates. (p. 148)

Once this disenchantment has come, and, of course, the earlier it comes the better, once the great illusion of the craft is understood and accepted, the lesson must never be forgotten, for it is forgotten only at maximum peril to the seaman and to his ship. In coping with a sea which is incapable of faith or trust, the seaman must be committed to unremitting vigilance, since the sea is swift and unforgiving in punishing any fall from grace. On this score, Conrad is quite adamant. In *The Mirror of the Sea,* he puts forth the only terms on which the seaman can hope to live with the sea:

For all that has been said of the love that certain natures (on shore) have professed to feel for it, for all the celebrations it has been the object of in prose and song, the sea has never been friendly to man. At most it has been the accomplice of human restlessness, and playing the part of dangerous abettor of world-wide ambitions. Faithful to no race after the manner of the kindly earth, receiving no impress from valor and toil and self-sacrifice, recognizing no finality of dominion, the sea has never adopted the cause of its masters like those lands where the victorious nations of mankind have taken root, rocking their cradles and setting up their grave-stones. He—man or people—who, putting his trust in the friendship of the sea, neglects the strength and cunning of his right hand, is a fool! (p. 135)

This is an extraordinary manifesto coming from a seaman, and it is interesting that the land, benighted though it may be in the seaman's eyes, fares so much better in the comparison which Conrad draws. By way of illustration of the necessity for the seaman to be always on guard, Conrad offers Mr. B—, the best of chief mates, as his demonstration piece. Curiously enough, Conrad seems to fault Mr. B— on this score, in that he depicts Mr. B— as overly vigilant. In a roundabout way, however, the fault is actually a central and saving virtue and the very basis for Conrad's admiration:

. . . of all my chief officers, the one I trusted most was a man called B—. . . . He was worth all his salt. . . . If it is permissible to criticize the absent, I should say he had a little too much of the sense of insecurity which is so invaluable in a seaman. He had an extremely disturbing air of being everlastingly ready (even when seated at table at my right hand before a plate of salt beef) to grapple with some impending calamity.
(The Mirror of the Sea, p. 18)

The sea's capacity for duplicity constitutes in itself an injustice, but the sea is capable of being unfair in other ways. The very terms under which men go to sea, for example, pitting one highly vulnerable ship and a handful of equally vulnerable men against the limitless might of the sea, represent a complete mismatch. The degree to which the odds are stacked against ship and men is perhaps best displayed in a passage from *Typhoon*. In speculating on the outcome of the confrontation between the *Nan-Shan* and the sea, Jukes, the first mate, is struck by the many ways in which the sea can win out and, consequently, the many challenges the ship must meet in order to survive:

If the steering-gear did not give way, if the immense volumes of water did not burst the deck in or smash one of the hatches, if the engines did not give up, if way could be kept on the ship against this terrific wind, and she did not bury herself in one of these awful seas, of whose white crests alone, topping high above her bows, he could now and then get a sickening glimpse—then there was a chance of her coming out of it. (p. 45)

So, too, in "Youth," the *Judea* faces impossible odds in the form of a sea whose force and fury is seemingly inexhaustible:

The sea was white like a sheet of foam, like a caldron of boiling milk; there was not a break in the clouds, no—not the size of a man's hand—no, not for so much as ten seconds. There was for us no sky, there were for us no stars, no sun, no universe—nothing but angry clouds and an infuriated sea. (p. 123)

In addition to the effect achieved by the vivid image of the frothing and seething of milk coming to a boil, the desperateness of the situation is underscored, in the passage, by the striking inversion of a Biblical allusion. The "little cloud no bigger than a man's hand" (I *Kings* 18:44) is a portent of the deluge to come. In Conrad's passage, however, the cloud cover is complete, the deluge has arrived, and there is not the slightest sign of a "little break" in the clouds, in other words, not the slightest hope of any abatement in the storm. And yet, the *Judea* endures; ultimately, it is the fire in her hold which destroys her and not the sea.

The *Judea* endures and so too do so many other ships and so many men in Conrad's sea tales. The capacity of ships and men to endure and to survive even against outrageous odds is the great fact and the great miracle of Conrad's sea world. Marlow, in reproaching Jim for not having had faith in the *Patna*, observes, "It's extraordinary what strains old iron will stand sometimes" (*Lord Jim*, p. 51). Marlow's pronouncement is, of course, in part euphemistic. "Old iron" refers not only to bulkheads and ships' hulls, but also to human hearts and human sinew and human nerves. It *is* extraordinary that the *Patna* and the *Narcissus* and the *Nan-Shan* endure, but it is even more extraordinary that such "old iron" as Singleton and MacWhirr and Allistoun and Whalley and, perhaps, Marlow himself also endure.

Conrad's sea, then, is a perfidious sea, a callous sea, a lawless sea which, recognizing no rules or standards, relishes an unfair fight. But it is also in Conrad, and most often, a cruel sea, an angry sea, and a monstrously violent sea.

The cruel sea has been a recurring theme in English literature from Beowulf to Nicholas Monsarrat, not surprising in view of the fact that English literature is the literature of an essentially seagoing race. Conrad, given due allowance for a certain chauvinism, is not far off the mark in the opening passage of "Youth" when he remarks of his story:

This could have occurred nowhere but in England, where men and sea interpenetrate, so to speak—the sea entering into the life of most men, and the men knowing something or everything about the sea, in the way of amusement, of travel, or of breadwinning.
(p. 115)

In all this thousand-year-and-more span of English literature of the sea, no writer has been as effective as Conrad in evoking the towering cruelty and the passionate anger of the sea. Conrad's success here results from the profound conviction manifest in his pages, a conviction born of direct observation. For, in whatever other guise the sea may appear in Conrad—occasionally benign, often deceitful, usually indifferent and usually unfair, it appears most frequently and most vividly in its cruelty.

In the sea tales, the cruelty of the sea is chiefly witnessed in scenes of storms at sea, which are something of a Conradian specialty. The depth of Conrad's apprehension and appreciation of the cruelty of the sea may be observed in the variety of devices he uses to render, as faithfully as possible, the unrestrained violence of a stormy and an angry sea.

There is, for example, the arresting image which Conrad employs to describe the advent of the gale in *The Nigger of the "Narcissus,"* an image which evokes precisely the sense of mindless and insane violence which he seeks to project:

A big, foaming sea came out of the mist; it made for the ship, roaring wildly, and in its rush it looked as mischievous and discomposing as a madman with an axe. (p. 343)

Something should be said of the stunning effect achieved in following up the two relatively innocuous modifiers, "mischievous" and "discomposing," with the startling "madman with an axe" which they modify.

There is the artful periodic structure of the passage in *Lord Jim* in which Marlow speaks of the sea's malevolence toward man. Conrad allows Marlow to disarm the reader by burying what he is getting at under a heavy coating of Marlovian rhetoric. The prick of the needle is thus sharper when, at the the end of the passage, the reader is brought up short by Marlow's matter-of-fact announcement that the intent of the sea is, quite simply, to kill:

There are many shades in the danger of adventures and gales, and it is only now and then that there appears on the face of facts a sinister violence of intention—that indefinable something which forces it upon the mind and the heart of a man, that this complication of accidents or these elemental furies are coming at him with a purpose of malice, with a strength beyond control, with an unbridled cruelty that means to tear out of him his hope and his fear, the pain of his fatigue and his longing for rest: which means to smash, to destroy, to annihilate all he has seen, known, loved, enjoyed, or hated; all that is priceless and necessary—the sunshine, the memories, the future; which means to sweep the whole precious world utterly away from his sight by the simple and appalling act of taking his life. (p. 7)

At times, Conrad, as if at a loss to describe the true force of the sea's violence, begs the issue and leaves the matter to the reader's imagination. This type of description, which is a kind of non-description, often proves extremely effective, as in the following passage from *Typhoon:*

Nobody—not even Captain MacWhirr, who alone on deck had caught sight of a white line of foam coming on at such a height that he couldn't believe his eyes—nobody was to know the steepness of that sea and the awful depth of the hollow the hurricane had scooped out behind the running wall of water. (p. 74)

Equally effective is the passage in *The Nigger of the "Narcissus"* wherein the destructive power of an angry sea is seen as cataclysmic, capable even of obliterating the very source of life, the sun:

To leeward, on the edge of the horizon, black seas leaped up towards the glowing sun. It sank slowly, round and blazing, and the crests of waves splashed on the edge of the luminous circle. . . the big seas began to roll across the crimson disc; and over miles of turbulent waters the shadows of high waves swept with a running darkness the faces of men. A crested roller broke with a loud hissing roar, and the sun, as if put out, disappeared. (p. 360)

In another passage from *The Nigger of the "Narcissus,"* the violence of the storm is pointed up not by describing the storm itself but by describing its effects. After the worst has passed and there is a moment of respite, the crew of the *Narcissus,* left with the legacy of the sea's violence, take stock of the pitiable remains:

The forecastle was a place of damp desolation. They looked at their dwelling with dismay. It was slimy, dripping; it hummed hollow with the wind, and was strewn with shapeless wreckage like a half-tide cavern in a rocky and exposed coast. Many had lost all they had in the world, but most of the starboard watch had preserved their chests; thin streams of water trickled out of them, however. The beds were soaked; the blankets spread out and saved by some nail squashed under foot. They dragged wet rags from evil-smelling corners, and, wringing the water out, recognized their property. (p. 378)

It must be particularly noted that the storm makes havoc of the order and systematic efficiency of the ship's routine which applies under normal conditions at sea. In fact, the aftermath of the storm strikingly resembles the handiwork of that other enemy of ships, the land. There is very little to choose between the chaos created by the storm and the chaos which prevails aboard a ship in dock.

But Conrad is nowhere more effective in evoking the violence of which the sea is capable than in a brief exchange which takes place between the captain in "The Secret Sharer" and Archbold, the skipper of the *Sephora.* Concerning the Leggatt affair, Archbold is at a total loss to comprehend what has happened to him and to his ship:

"I have been at sea now, man and boy, for seven-and-thirty years, and I've never heard of such a thing happening in an English ship. And that it should be my ship. Wife on board, too."
I was hardly listening to him.
"Don't you think . . . that the heavy sea which, you told me, came aboard just then might have killed the man? I have seen the sheer weight of a sea kill a man very neatly, by simply breaking his neck."

(p. 674)

Essentially, the conversation between the two has nothing really to do with the cruelty or the violence of the sea. Its chief purpose is to demonstrate the extent to which the young captain is committed to Leggatt, since he seeks some way of excusing and, perhaps, condoning Leggatt's action in strangling a member of the *Sephora*'s crew. But the captain's laconic comment which closes the exchange horrifies the reader and opens up to him, in the fullest measure, the awesome destructive power of the sea in its violence.

The cruelty of the sea toward the seaman, however, goes beyond the somewhat straightforward act of taking his life or destroying his ship. The sea practices another and much more subtle form of cruelty. It robs the seaman of the power of sight.

Inured as we are, here in the twentieth century, to such sophisticated detection devices as radar and sonar and loran, it is not possible for us to appreciate how vital the ability to see clearly was for the men in the clipper ships of Conrad's day, just a century ago. It was, quite literally, a matter of life or death, and not only was the seaman's existence at stake, but, equally literally, the survival of the ship lay at hazard. Indeed, the terms of survival at sea have not really changed; it is just that the odds have been considerably reduced today. Modern scanning devices are, in effect, complementary eyes; they are man's response to the sea's challenge and they represent a largely successful effort to compensate for the handicaps under which the sea can place him, if it chooses to do so.

In Conrad's time, the odds were heavily balanced in favor of the sea (yet another instance of the sea's unwillingness to play fair), and Conrad had a full appreciation of the dangers created by this disparity. The life-and-death nature of the seaman's need to see clearly dominates the following passage from *The Mirror of the Sea*, a passage which is characterized by an intensity of feeling that is rare even for the naturally emotional Conrad:

To see! to see!—this is the craving of the sailor, as of the rest of blind humanity. To have his path made clear for him is the aspiration of every human being in our beclouded and tempestuous existence. I have heard a reserved, silent man, with no nerves to speak of, after three days of hard running in thick south-westerly weather, burst out passionately: "I wish to God we could get sight of something!" (p. 87)

The vital need to see and its obverse, the maliciousness of the sea in blinding the seaman, are recurring themes throughout Conrad's sea tales. In *Typhoon*, for instance, the issue is raised at several points. At the first warning of the hurricane, Jukes, the chief mate, who has been inwardly amused at his captain's eccentricities and who fancies himself as the complete sailor, is alone on deck. Within moments, MacWhirr, faithful always to the demands of his calling, appears on the bridge, and Jukes discovers, in Conrad's words, that he is "uncritically glad to have his captain at hand" (p. 39), or, to put it another way without distorting the context, to have him in sight. When the full force of the hurricane hits, its chief effect is the immediate loss of visual power. Conrad puts it this way in a key statement, not only for this story and this storm, but for all of Conrad's storms at sea:

It was something formidable and swift, like the sudden smashing of a vial of wrath. It seemed to explode all round the ship with an overpowering concussion and a rush of great waters, as if an immense dam had been blown up to windward. In an instant the men lost touch of each other. This is the disintegrating power of a great wind: it isolates one from one's kind. (*Typhoon*, p. 40)

The storm "isolates one from one's kind" largely by robbing him of visual contact with others who are in the same situation. Marlow, in another context (*Lord Jim*, p. 14) says, "In our own hearts we trust for our salvation in the men that surround us, in the sights that fill our eyes, in the sounds that fill our ears, and in the air that fills our lungs." Jukes is a fine exemplar of the validity of Marlow's observation. A brave man in all respects, Jukes undergoes a temporary funk when he is sent below to survey the pandemonium which has broken out among the coolies on the 'tween-deck. Here, deprived of the comforting presence of men around him, unable to see another of his kind, Jukes nearly loses his nerve. And Jukes is afflicted by another kind of faulty vision, the inability of the mind to see and to comprehend:

Jukes was driven away from his commander. He fancied himself whirled a great distance through the air. Everything disappeared— even, for a moment, his power of thinking. . . . His distress was by no means alleviated by an inclination to disbelieve the reality of this experience. Though young, he had seen some bad weather, and had never doubted his ability to imagine the worst; but this was so much beyond his powers of fancy that it appeared incompatible with the existence of any ship whatever. (p. 41)

If it is important for Jukes to be able to see or, for that matter, any member of the crew of the *Nan-Shan* to be able to see, it is absolutely imperative that MacWhirr's vision should not be impaired. If the sea is unfair and cruel in isolating "one from one's kind," it is never more cruel nor more unfair than when it isolates the captain from his ship. It is true, of course, that a ship's captain is better prepared and better equipped to function in isolation. In effect, he does this all the time. But the solitary judgments which a captain must make are normally carefully considered judgments, based on the facts as he sees them. During the hurricane in *Typhoon*, MacWhirr cannot see the facts; he cannot see his ship clearly, and he chafes under the marked disadvantage at which the sea has placed him:

The sea, flattened down in the heavier gusts, would uprise and overwhelm both ends of the *Nan-Shan* in snowy rushes of foam, expanding wide, beyond both rails, into the night. And on this dazzling sheet, spread under the blackness of the clouds and emitting a bluish glow, Captain MacWhirr could catch a desolate glimpse of a few tiny specks black as ebony, the tops of the hatches, the battened companions, the heads of the covered winches, the foot of a mast. This was all he could see of his ship. (p. 43)

Later, at the height of the storm, MacWhirr's voice is heard from the bridge through the engine room speaking tube, and the words are the plaintive cry of a man who must see and who has been

rendered blind: "Dark and rain. Can't see what's coming. . . .
Must—keep—her—moving—enough to steer—and chance it"
(p. 67). In this context, we might refer to a passage quoted earlier
in conjunction with the discussion of the violence of the sea.
MacWhirr, it will be recalled, catches sight of an enormous wave
breaking toward the ship, and we are told that "he couldn't believe his eyes." Like Jukes, MacWhirr is the victim of this special
form of impaired vision—the inability of the mind to comprehend what the eyes see.

"The Secret Sharer" comes naturally to mind in enumerating
examples, in Conrad, of the sea's capacity for depriving the
seaman of the one indispensable faculty at sea, his power of sight.
The young captain in the story, in bringing his ship close in to
Koh-ring, cannot see where he is in relation to the island's reefs,
which are ready to tear the bottom out of his vessel. The tension
of the moment is admirably captured in a brief exchange between
the captain and the helmsman, the man whose ability to see is
next in importance to the captain's:

"Keep her full. Don't check her way. That won't do now," I said
warningly.
"I can't see the sails very well," the helmsman answered me, in
strange, quavering tones. (p. 696)

The helmsman's reply, it will be noted, comes in a "strange"
voice, the strained voice of a man who must see to steer and who
recognizes that he can neither see nor steer very well.

In the same story, the degree of peril involved in being
sightless at sea is effectively dramatized through the medium of
the chief mate. His characteristic response to virtually any situation is the vague and bland, "Bless my soul." When, however, he
steps onto the bridge just as the ship is closing on the island, the
absolute inability to see and the dangerous proximity of the land
in the darkness, wrings from the mate the agonized cry, "My
God! Where are we?" (p. 696).

Jim is afflicted with a rather peculiar form of faulty vision
in that he sees too much. In Jim's case, the mind's eye of his
imagination accepts and assimilates more than does his normal
channel of vision. The trouble here is that the imagination is
creative, or, to continue the ocular metaphor, the imagination is

a flawed mirror; it enlarges and distorts. In a way, that superb visionary of *Lord Jim,* Chester, is right. Jim doesn't see things "exactly as they are" (p. 99). Two instances may be cited wherein Jim doesn't see things clearly or doesn't see what is really there: his eyes betray him as to the extent of the damage to the *Patna*'s bulkhead, and, as a result of having misseen or misinterpreted the facts, the judgment he comes to proves fatal; second, Jim shares the delusion of the others in the *Patna*'s lifeboat that they have seen the ship's lights disappear into the water, and their eyes deceive them into believing that the *Patna* has gone down.

In another instance, Jim sees not too much but, instead, nothing at all. It will be remembered that during the last minutes on the *Patna,* Jim shuts his eyes in order to blot out the "funny sight" of the desperate efforts of the other white men trying to launch one of the ship's boats. But this works to his disadvantage, for when Jim closes his eyes the imaginative sight takes over. Paradoxically, Jim is equally blind with his eyes open or shut.

In *Heart of Darkness,* Marlow discovers that even though his vessel is far inland, two hundred miles from the sea, the same essential conditions apply among men and boats and water—the seaman's prime requisite continues to be his need to see. In fact, given the myriad snags in the river, the tricky currents, and the precarious state of his rickety steamboat, Marlow's eyes must be everywhere at once. The voyage upriver to Kurtz's station provides Marlow with a comprehensive examination in inland seamanship and navigation. And the river is not the only source of danger. As the boat moves deeper into the heart of darkness, Marlow, an essentially honest man, admits to feeling "the fascination of the abomination" (p. 6). And the reason he doesn't go ashore for "a howl and a dance" (p. 37) has, as he puts it, nothing to do with principles; he is simply too busy looking ahead and trying to keep his boat off the banks of the river. Even at the highly dramatic and highly distracting moment when the helmsman leaves the wheel, fires the Martini-Henry out the window, and lurches back clutching a spear imbedded in his ribs, Marlow remains at his post, although with difficulty: "I had to make an effort to free my eyes from his gaze and attend to the steering" (p. 47).

In view of Marlow's dedication to the job at hand, a dedication maintained amidst distractions enough to unseat most men, it is manifestly cruel and unfair that Marlow be further burdened with the seaman's particular nemesis, fog. The sea, in this case its subsidiary, the river, has many ways of limiting the seaman's vision—blinding rain, mist, snow, sleet, darkness—but none so effective as fog. With the arrival of the early morning fog, Marlow's blindness is total, so much so that he is forced to do what no seaman will do except under the most dire circumstances; he stops his boat dead in the water. The totality of Marlow's blindness is vividly displayed in the following passage, chiefly through the fine sensory appeal of the opening sentence and the conciseness and concreteness of the shutter image:

When the sun rose there was a white fog, very warm and clammy, and more blinding than the night. It did not shift or drive; it was just there standing all round you like something solid. At eight or nine, perhaps, it lifted as a shutter lifts. We had a glimpse of the towering multitude of trees, of the immense matted jungle, with the blazing little ball of the sun hanging over it—all perfectly still —and then the white shutter came down again, smoothly, as if sliding in greased grooves. (p. 40)

Marlow confesses the gravity of his situation in another passage which becomes a kind of grudging tribute to the fog's power to render him sightless and, thus, helpless:

Keep a look-out? Well, you may guess I watched the fog for the signs of lifting as a cat watches a mouse; but for anything else our eyes were of no more use to us than if we had been buried miles deep in a heap of cotton-wool. (p. 44)

And the whole issue of the seaman's need to see, of his helplessness in being blind, of the power of the fog virtually to transform the world into something unrecognizable, unknown, and, therefore, deadly, is summed up in this, Marlow's view from the pilot house:

What we could see was just the steamer we were on, her outlines blurred as though she had been on the point of dissolving, and a misty strip of water, perhaps two feet broad, around her—and that was all. The rest of the world was nowhere, as far as our eyes and ears were concerned. Just nowhere. Gone, disappeared; swept off without leaving a whisper or a shadow behind. (pp. 40–41)

One of Conrad's favorite adjectives, occurring next in frequency to "immense" and "luminous," is "palpable." The term is warranted here; it is no exaggeration to say that in chronicling the passage of the steamboat up the Congo, Conrad has made wholly palpable the feeling of fog and its power to stifle the senses, especially the sense of sight.

The most dramatic example, in Conrad, of a seaman unable to see is Captain Whalley in *The End of the Tether*. Unlike the visual problems described thus far, Whalley's impaired vision is not figurative or temporary; he is going blind, quite literally, and only his devotion to his daughter keeps him at sea. Ultimately, the sea extracts the full price for his folly and herein Whalley epitomizes the dangers inherent in a seaman's loss of sight. The sea is hardly culpable for Whalley's impending blindness, but, at the same time, it is the sea, in conspiracy with Massy, which brings about Whalley's undoing. For, before reaching out and destroying him, the sea has allowed Whalley to believe that the most dangerous game he is playing will work. And the sea does not hesitate to capitalize on Whalley's point of weakness, his blindness, the blindness which makes him vulnerable. Clearly, a sighted Whalley would have made all the difference. Had Whalley been able to see the landmarks which had become familiar to him in three years of piloting the *Sofala* over the same route, no amount of tampering with the compass could have deceived him. Instead, he is blind to his surroundings and forced to rely on the evidence of the compass, which he *can* see. As a result, the *Sofala* ends up on the reef and Whalley suffers the seaman's final degradation, losing a ship.

It is noteworthy that the only one of Conrad's seamen who professes to be able to see clearly, who, in fact, boasts of his vision, sees nothing but hallucinations. The chief engineer of the *Patna,* in *Lord Jim,* the "old stager" whom Marlow encounters in the hospital, assures Marlow "Only my eyes were good enough to see. I am famous for my eyesight" (p. 32). The reference is to seeing the running lights of the *Patna* going down into the water, since it is largely on the engineer's testimony that the others are convinced the *Patna* has sunk. What the engineer chiefly sees, in his advanced state of delirium tremens, is toads, by Jove—to use the Marlovian, under his bed, on the covers, all about him. The degree of reliability of the engineer's ocular powers is best evidenced by the doctor's dry reference to his "batrachian visions" (p. 34) and Marlow's dismissal of the testimony which the engineer might give at the inquiry as "not in the least material" (p. 34).

"To see! to see!" Conrad has said, and the cry recalls Conrad's insistence elsewhere on the need to see. There is, for instance, the widely quoted passage from the "Preface" to *The Nigger of the "Narcissus"* in which Conrad says that the artist's task is "before all, to make you *see*." There is Marlow's obsession in both *Lord Jim* and *Heart of Darkness* with his inability to "see" the central figures clearly enough and, in turn, his inability to let his auditors see properly. Thus, there are sufficient grounds for advancing the argument that the need to see is of a piece in all of these instances. The seaman's need to see is the physical and temporal counterpart of Marlow's (and of Conrad's) desire both to see and to make seen, in the spiritual and non-temporal sense. In both cases, the end sought is substantially the same. The seaman must see clearly in order to understand his situation and judge correctly; in like fashion, the writer (or narrator) must have clear sight in order that his audience may understand fully and judge correctly.

We might return to the main thesis of this chapter by raising the question, what is the seaman's attitude toward the sea? In the passage quoted earlier from *The Mirror of the Sea,* in which Conrad reveals the depths of the sea's capacity for deceit, one stance is suggested. Having issued the warning that the man who places his faith in the sea is a fool, Cnorad goes on to say: *"Odi et amo* may well be the confession of those who consciously or blindly have surrendered their existence to the fascination of the sea" (p. 135). The seaman's (and Conrad's) attitude would thus appear to be ambiguous, running the full range from love to hate at times, but existing, at most times, as an admixture of the two emotions. There is, however, one common point at which all of Conrad's seamen—Singleton, Lingard, the captain of "The Secret Sharer," Jukes, Marlow—seem to meet. All of them have learned or come to learn never to trust the sea.

CHAPTER THREE

THE SHIPS

No ship is wholly bad.   —*The Mirror of the Sea*

"Ships!" exclaimed an elderly seaman . . . "ships are all right; it's the men in 'em."   —*The Mirror of the Sea*

"You will go into steam presently. Everybody goes into steam."   —*A Personal Record*

In the section of *The Mirror of the Sea* which Conrad devotes to his continuing romance with the Mediterranean, "the Nursery of the Craft," as he calls it, Conrad indulges in some fanciful speculation on the origins of the seafaring life. He postulates one particularly resolute member of the early tribes that inhabited the Mediterranean shores who finds his landlocked life intolerable. This "adventurous and shaggy ancestor" (p. 149), placing his faith in the stoutness of a primitive wooden hull, sets forth on the water and accomplishes "the first coasting trip in a sheltered bay ringing with the admiring howls of his tribe" (p. 149). In the centuries which have passed, ships have become more sophisticated and seamen more knowledgeable, but, in the essentials, nothing has really changed. The seaman today, like his daring ancestor, still puts his entire trust in his ship and, secure in its seaworthiness and its integrity, goes to sea.

The seaman's trust is well placed. In all of Conrad, there is not a single instance of a faithless ship. The land, as we have seen, may be presumed to be deceitful; the sea may be expected to be deceitful; but a ship, never. Thus, in Conrad's attitude toward ships and, since we have been equating created with creator throughout this study, presumably in his seamen's attitude toward ships, there is nothing of the ambivalence, the ambiguity, and the equivocation to be found in their responses to the land and to the sea. The seaman trusts his ship of a right and with a surety.

The theme of the fidelity of ships occurs with such frequency in Conrad's sea tales that one is pressed to select the best instance, among many, where the statement is put forth. Perhaps the most fruitful method of attack will be to demonstrate that the faithfulness of ships is a conviction which is shared by both Conrad and all of Conrad's seamen, from the very best of the calling to the very least.

As for Conrad himself, his testament to the steadfastness of ships is heard many times in the autobiographical *The Mirror of the Sea*. It is nowhere heard more clearly, however, nor more convincingly than in the following passage, a view of the ships and docks of London, in which Conrad touches upon the motif of the ship as a prisoner of the land once more and then enlarges upon it:

As you pass alongside each hopeless prisoner chained to the quay, the slight grinding noise of the wooden fenders makes a sound of angry muttering. But, after all, it may be good for ships to go through a period of restraint and repose, as the restraint and self-communion of inactivity may be good for an unruly soul—not, indeed, that I mean to say that ships are unruly; on the contrary, they are faithful creatures, as so many men can testify. And faithfulness is a great restraint, the strongest bond laid upon the self-will of men and ships on this globe of land and sea. (pp. 110–11)

It is significant that, in this passage, Conrad links what are for him the two chief virtues, fidelity and restraint. It will be recalled that restraint is a central theme in *Heart of Darkness.* Marlow's restraint, for example, is, according to his own somewhat arcane testimony, largely to be found in the form of the rivets that he needs to repair the steamboat. And the nearest Marlow comes to a final judgment on Kurtz is his equally cryptic assertion that "rivets were what really Mr. Kurtz wanted, if he had only known it" (p. 29).

But, restraint is not the private desideratum of Marlow or Kurtz or of the other white men in the Congo. Restraint is crucial for all men, the savage as well as the civilized. For instance, Marlow is filled with admiration for the restraint exhibited by the cannibals whom the company hires as woodcutters to supply the steamboat on the journey to Kurtz's station. On the other hand, the native helmsman who dashes to the pilot house window to make his contribution to the chaos when the boat is attacked clearly lacks restraint and suffers for it. The statement Conrad would make is that those who exercise restraint, like Marlow and like the cannibals, survive; those who lack restraint, like Kurtz and like the helmsman, perish. And it is only a slight oversimplification to say that restraint, or the lack of it, lies at the heart of most on Conrad's sea tales and is the determinant in the success or failure of most of his seamen. Jim, for example, lacks restraint in giving full play to his destructive imagination; Lingard lacks restraint in seeking to play God ashore and, in both instances, the common failing leads to disaster. Conversely, MacWhirr meets the challenge of the hurricane with admirable restraint; and Beard, in his insistence on heading the burning, virtually derelict *Judea* toward her original destination, Bangkok, displays almost classic restraint. In these two last instances, the presence of restraint is a positive saving grace. Restraint, then, and the virtue which Conrad makes its corollary, fidelity, are fundamental matters with Conrad, and to say that a ship is faithful is to give it the highest kind of praise.

The best statement about a ship's fidelity to be found in *The Rescue* is a bit more imaginative, but nonetheless it rings of conviction. In a moment of idleness, Lingard meditates on the many attributes of his brig *Lightning:*

To him she was as full of life as the great world. He felt her live in every motion, in every roll, in every sway of her tapering masts, of those masts whose painted trucks move forever, to a seaman's eye, against the clouds or against the stars. To him she was always precious—like old love; always desirable—like a strange woman; always tender—like a mother; always faithful—like the favorite daughter of a man's heart. (p. 10)

Two points should be remarked in this passage: first, that the climactic order in which the *Lightning*'s virtues are enumerated places the emphasis where Conrad would have it—on the chief of the brig's attributes, her fidelity; second, that although this is the *Lightning* as seen through Lingard's eyes, putting the fiction of explicit-implicit narrator aside for the moment, the voice speaking is Conrad's. Or, even if the distinction between writer and persona is preserved, in view of the evidence of the passage quoted from *The Mirror of the Sea,* there is still no reason to believe that the two, Lingard and Conrad, would not speak with one voice.

The most moving and most memorable tribute to the fidelity of ships comes, paradoxically, from the least articulate of Conrad's seamen, the patriarchal Singleton. Actually, it would be more accurate to call Singleton the least articulate of Conrad's seamen on every subject except that of the sea. On one of the few occasions in *The Nigger of the "Narcissus"* when Singleton deigns to exchange words with Jimmy Wait, he is pressed by Wait for an opinion on the seaworthiness of the *Narcissus.* This is, of course, an unseamanlike question and a totally pointless one to address to the man who embodies, for Conrad, all that is best in the calling. Singleton, we are told, "didn't stir. A long while after he said, with unmoved face: 'Ship! . . . Ships are all right. It is the men in them!' " (p. 312). The episode provides further evidence for the conviction already expressed in this book that there is a consanguinity of thinking between creator and created in many of Conrad's sea tales. Singleton's remark grew out of a real-life incident in which Conrad was involved. The line is, in fact, a slightly emended version of the words which Conrad heard an old seaman utter while the two shared a moment of the fellowship of the craft, gazing at the rows of ships in the New South Dock in London: "Ships! . . . Ships . . . ships are all right; it's the men in 'em" (*The Mirror of the Sea,* pp. 128–29). I have termed Singleton's testimonial to ships "memorable." Its power to stick in the mind is evidenced by the fact that Conrad did remember the remark over the years and later put it into the mouth of the most worthy of his seamen. That same memorable quality renders it fitting as an epigraph to this chapter.

But one would naturally expect Singleton, the best of seamen, to speak favorably of a ship. One would not, however, expect to hear such appreciation from one of the least worthy of Conrad's seamen, and the fact that we do, in *The Rescue,* suggests the universality of the ship's reputation for being trustworthy. Shaw, Lingard's second-in-command aboard the *Lightning,* is a far cry from the best of chief mates, Mr. B——. Shaw is, in fact, one of Conrad's losers among seamen, men who, either by temperament or incompetence or by sheer bad luck, are fated never to achieve command, the ultimate recognition of a seaman's worthiness. Shaw, protesting that he is "a respectable man . . . married . . . had children . . . a peaceable man" (p. 189), is horrified by Lingard's extralegal methods and by his disdain toward doing things by the book. When the complication of the stranded yacht *Hermit* and the influential Mr. Travers comes up, Shaw can contain himself no longer and remonstrates with Lingard: he (Shaw) "followed the sea respectably out and home, all regular, not vagabonding here and there, chumming with the first nigger that came along and laying traps for his betters" (p. 190). Shaw, of course, is chiefly concerned with the immense harm or good which Mr. Travers can do him. The tininess of Shaw's mind and his inordinate self-righteousness (not to mention his craven nature) are made explicit by Conrad in a passage wherein the diction employed plays a central role:

It was a moral aspiration, but in his alarm the native grossness of his nature came clattering out like a devil out of a trap. He would blow the gaff, split, give away the whole show . . . say what he thought, let all the world know . . . he washed his hands of everything. (p. 191)

And then, there is this remarkable exchange:

"And the brig?" asked Lingard, suddenly.
Shaw was checked. For a second the seaman in him instinctively admitted the claim of the ship.
"The brig. The brig. She's right enough. . . . He had nothing to say against the brig—not he." (p. 191)

The point is well made by Conrad. For all his protestations and denunciations, even Shaw, the least of seamen, is still seaman enough to preserve the sanctity of the ship. Although they are otherwise eons apart, Singleton and Shaw can meet on the common ground shared by all seamen, their belief in the fidelity of the ship. (In this context, it might be recalled that even Donkin, who is depraved enough a seaman to countenance mutiny, has nothing unkind to say about the *Narcissus.*)

Singleton's laconic testimony to the ship's capacity for faithfulness raises an issue which is encountered at several junctures in Conrad's sea tales. "Ships are all right," Singleton has said, "it's the men in them." The clear implication here is that ships are always blameless, are always to be exonerated and held guiltless. In other words, in the event of failure, it is not the ship which is culpable, but the men who serve her. In point of fact, the thesis that ships are ever innocent of blame is much more than implied in Conrad; it is an article of faith openly professed, adamantly championed, and always to be subscribed to.

For example, in *The Mirror of the Sea,* Conrad returns to the note struck by Singleton's forerunner, the elderly seaman, and sounds it again, as if he fears either that the ship's innocence has not been fully stated or that it cannot be stated fully enough:

"Ships are all right." They are. They who live with the sea have got to hold by that creed first and last. (p. 147)

The force of the positive and all-encompassing assertion, "first and last," should not be overlooked, since such total conviction is rather rare in Conrad. Nor should the preciseness of Conrad's use of "creed," as opposed, for example, to "faith." "Faith" is more general and somewhat abstract; "creed," on the other hand, is quite concrete and explicit. A creed is the central statement of one's faith, and the conclusion which must be reached here is that the seaman need accept only this one tenet, that ships are "all right," to be provided with a working code by which he may live and survive.

Elsewhere in *The Mirror of the Sea,* the thesis that ships are "all right" is met again in the course of Conrad's reminiscences of what was for him the nonpareil of ships, the balancelle *Tremolino.* "I am," Conrad asserts, "concerned but for the good name of the *Tremolino* and I affirm that a ship is ever guiltless of the sins, transgressions, and follies of her men" (p. 161). It may be objected that since Conrad is speaking of the *Tremolino,* his judgment might be impaired by a sentimentality or a nostalgia which leads him to excess. But, if the passage is read carefully, it becomes evident that, in Conrad's mind, what is true of the *Tremolino* is true of all ships. Conrad does, of course, have the *Tremolino* in mind, but it will be noted that he uses the indefinite, "a ship," rather than the specific, "this ship," that is, the *Tremolino.*

But perhaps the most emphatic assertion of the ship's freedom from guilt is to be found in yet another passage from *The Mirror of the Sea,* a passage which begins with the unequivocal affirmation used as an epigraph to this chapter, then comes full circle and closes with an equally forceful restatement of the ship's innocence:

No ship is wholly bad; and now that their bodies that had braved so many tempests have been blown off the face of the sea by a puff of steam, the evil and the good together into the limbo of things that have served their time, there can be no harm in affirming that in these vanished generations of willing servants there never has been one utterly unredeemable soul. (pp. 119–20)

Decisive in tone as this passage seems to be, however, it does open up some problems. The qualifying "wholly" of the first sentence and the phrase "utterly unredeemable" of the last sentence leave room for relative guilt or innocence, and, in putting forth his thesis of a ship's blamelessness, Conrad has been talking in absolutes. The contradiction is, I submit, more apparent than real, though its resolution is by no means transparent. The reasoning goes something like this: Conrad does not say that ships are perfect; he knew them too well to be guilty of so manifest an oversimplification. There are, Conrad readily admits, flawed ships—"the cranky, the lazy, the wet, the bad sea boats, the wild steerers, the capricious, the pig-headed, the generally ungovernable" (*The Mirror of the Sea,* p. 119). But, whatever their imperfections and idiosyncrasies, ships are essentially the "servants" of men (the term occurs again and again in Conrad) and under man's governance. In Conrad's mind, the issue is not one of bad servants but bad masters. The servants, to continue Conrad's metaphor, are often badly served by their masters, who fail to make provision for the ship's shortcomings or who demand more of a ship than she is capable of giving. By this method of rationalization, the one that Conrad subscribes to, Singleton's verdict holds. In cases of failure, it is the men who are at fault; the ship's integrity remains intact. The ship, in other words, is a constant; the men who put to sea in her are the variables.

A specific example of a flawed but guiltless ship will contribute much toward an understanding of this admittedly complex point. The *Narcissus* is a flawed ship. Because of her design (a matter of man's and not the ship's choosing, it should be noted), she is prone to be unstable and wants the nicest handling in loading. The narrator of *The Nigger of the "Narcissus,"* in a passage which is largely a paean of praise for his ship, admits her fault, but he does so with a certain defensiveness that borders on admiration:

We all watched her. She was beautiful and had a weakness. We loved her no less for that. We admired her qualities aloud, we boasted of them to one another, as though they had been our own, and the consciousness of her only fault we kept buried in the silence of our profound affection. She was born in the thundering peal of hammers beating upon iron, in black eddies of smoke, under a gray sky, on the banks of the Clyde. The clamorous and somber stream gives birth to things of beauty that float away into the sunshine of the world to be loved by men. The *Narcissus* was one of that perfect brood. Less perfect than many perhaps, but she was ours, and, consequently, incomparable. . . . We knew she was the most magnificent sea boat ever launched. We tried to forget that, like many good sea boats, she was at times rather crank. She was exacting. She wanted care in loading and handling, and no one knew exactly how much care would be enough. Such are the imperfections of mere men! The ship knew, and sometimes would correct the presumptuous human ignorance by the wholesome discipline of fear. (pp. 336-37)

The point to be stressed here, because it is the point which the narrator stresses, is that the *Narcissus*'s instability is man's fault and man's problem and if she is not loaded properly, it is man's imperfection and not the ship's. Conrad is unusually vehement because he was writing from actual experience. The real life counterpart of the *Narcissus*, as far as the ship's instability is concerned, was the *Highland Forest*, a ship in which Conrad sailed from Amsterdam to Samarang in 1887. It was also the first ship in which Conrad served as first mate and, thus, the first ship in which he functioned as chief cargo officer. In his ignorance of the *Highland Forest*'s peculiarities and special needs, the new mate loaded her by the book, keeping the weight well up, "one third of the whole being in the upper part 'above the beams' " (*The Mirror of the Sea*, p. 52). Ironically, in doing so, Conrad had made his ship too stable and had created a seagoing rocking horse. Conrad's captain, the prototype of MacWhirr, in an effort to be diplomatic, ventures to predict, "Well, we shall have a lively time of it this passage, I bet" (p. 53). Lively, but not comfortable, since, as Conrad ruefully sums up, "No seaman can feel comfortable in body or mind when he has made his ship uneasy" (p. 53).

With a view of further clarifying Conrad's insistence on the sanctity of the ship, it might be instructive to examine three ships in the sea stories that serve better than they are served. It might also be worthwhile to note that in two instances, *Lord Jim* and *The End of the Tether*, the ships that have been misserved exact an immediate and demanding retribution. In the third case, "Youth," a special set of circumstances applies.

The *Patna* is scarcely the seaman's *beau ideal* among ships, but, at the same time, she scarcely deserves to be served as she is in being basely abandoned at sea by her ignoble crew. And among these latter, for the moment at least, Jim must be included. In contrast to the crew's dereliction, the *Patna* remains faithful to her trust, as Singleton, as Conrad, as any worthy seaman would have anticipated. The *Patna* completes her appointed task; she stays afloat and she does make port, even though at the end of a tow line.

For his apostasy, Jim is dealt an exacting punishment which carries with it a kind of poetic justice. Having placed a stigma on the *Patna* in deserting her, Jim, in turn, must carry the stigma of the *Patna* with him to the very moment when the old nakhoda, Doramin, levels his pistol at Jim's chest on Patusan. It could be said, with considerable validity, that Jim betrays the *Patna* once, but the *Patna* betrays Jim, or, better still, causes Jim to betray himself, for the remainder of his life.

One might argue that in singling Jim out for punishment,

destiny or Providence or the fates are manifestly unfair. The rest of the *Patna*'s crew, after all, emerge unscathed. But, the rest of the crew don't matter; it is only Jim who is of consequence, or, at least, so Marlow has insisted with the refrain-like pronouncement, "He is one of us," which is repeated throughout the novel. Jim is of consequence chiefly in that he is of the fellowship of the craft, and herein lies the crux of the matter. Jim's punishment is indeed unfair under any standards except those of the world he inhabits, Conrad's sea world, in which the craft sets extremely rigorous guidelines. Such are the special sanctions of this world that Jim's culpability and his punishment are conditions and consequences of being a member of the fellowship. Of the *Patna*'s crew, only Jim is worthy; only he has pledged his faith to ships, and only he really breaks faith. As for the rest of the crew, Conrad's position would be that where there is no faith to begin with, there can be no breach of faith.

The *Sofala*, in *The End of the Tether*, is another of Conrad's ships that is poorly served. The most immediate sin committed against her is, of course, Massy's tampering with the compass, which sends the *Sofala* to the bottom. Here again, Singleton's dictum stands; the *Sofala* is all right, it's the men aboard her who bring her to grief. The *Sofala* steers faithfully on the course set for her, placing her security in the mutual trust between ships and seamen and, guiltless, steers to her own destruction.

If Massy is the immediate cause of the *Sofala*'s downfall, the ultimate and the most heinous offender is Captain Whalley. His offense actually begins before Massy takes action. Whalley continues to take the *Sofala* to sea even after he is well aware of his impending blindness. In effect, in placing his daughter's welfare before that of his ship, Whalley is using the *Sofala* for his own ends. He serves the *Sofala* very badly indeed since, each time he goes to sea half-blind, he violates the tacit accord between ships and men and exposes his ship to ever increasing risks. Finally, Whalley risks too much, and the *Sofala*'s fate must be squarely charged to Whalley's account; for if Whalley had been able to see the landmarks about him, Massy's doctoring would have been detected and the ship put back on course.

The same apparent disparity in the punishment meted out

that we observed in Jim's case may be seen again in the *Sofala* affair. Whalley is punished in the most telling manner possible for a seaman. It is not so much that he goes down with his ship; this, after all, is in keeping with the traditional code of the sea. Nor is it really that Whalley has lost a ship, although this would normally be sufficient punishment for a seaman, and a master seaman at that. Rather, the cruelest cut is that Whalley is fated to die in the knowledge that his ship has been betrayed and that he, the master, has played a central role in that betrayal. Massy, on the other hand, equally guilty by both moral and temporal law, gets off scot-free; he will collect the insurance indemnity and will, presumably, live and prosper. But the disparity here may be resolved as it was in *Lord Jim*. Like the *Patna*'s crew, Jim excepted, Massy is of no consequence. Only Whalley belongs to the fellowship and only Whalley has genuinely broken faith, or, for that matter, is capable of breaking faith.

The case of the *Judea* in "Youth" is much more complex. It would seem, in fact, to be an exception to Singleton's rule. The *Judea* appears to be a pariah among ships, a ship that is not "all right," a ship that serves badly. Seemingly apropos of nothing, she springs a leak shortly after her departure for Bangkok and the men aboard her are forced to return to port. On her second attempt, a fire breaks out in the *Judea*'s hold, a fire which proves mortal, and the men aboard her are forced to abandon ship. That the fire is attributed to spontaneous combustion appears to be further evidence of the ship's intransigence. The *Judea*, in allowing the sea to penetrate her hull and, later, in engendering the fire, seems to be intent on destroying herself, a clear breach of the faith which men have come to place in all ships. Singleton's rule seems to be abrogated categorically here, since not only is the *Judea* not "all right," but there is also nothing wrong with the men in her. The *Judea* is very well served by her captain and her crew. Until the final moment when they have no choice but to leave the ship, their combined efforts and energies are directed toward keeping the *Judea* afloat and headed for her appointed destination, Bangkok.

In point of fact, however, none of the "seems" enumerated

has any basis in reality. The *Judea* can be readily exonerated, and her case is an exception only in that both the ship and the men on her are faithful. The *Judea,* it will be recalled, does keep faith, continuing "do or die" on her course for Bangkok until, on fire from bow to stern, she can go no farther and lies dead in the water. The *Judea*'s fidelity and her innocence of fault are attested to by the fact that she is blessed with an heroic burial at sea, a burial befitting a worthy ship. Quite noticeably, one of the most effective passages in "Youth" is Conrad's description of the *Judea*'s viking-like funeral:

A high, clear flame, an immense and lonely flame, ascended from the ocean, and from its summit the black smoke poured continuously at the sky. She burned furiously; mournful and imposing like a funeral pile kindled in the night, surrounded by the sea, watched over by the stars. A magnificent death had come like a grace, like a gift, like a reward to that old ship at the end of her laborious days. (p. 146)

The steadfastness of the captain and crew is, in turn, certified several times in the story by Marlow, and it is reflected in the rewards and punishments that are assigned.

If the *Judea* has been well served by the men aboard her, she has been poorly served by the men on land—the owners, the underwriters—who have kept her too long at sea. Or, to put it in more precise terms, the men ashore have asked more of the *Judea* than she is capable of giving. She is simply not fit for the sea, and the fact that she springs a leak is a predictable consequence of man's shortcomings and shortsightedness, and not the ship's. So too, the fire, in all fairness, must be ascribed to men's actions. The ideal conditions for its outbreak are created when the cargo is loaded and unloaded too many times while the ship is in port. As a result of these multiple handlings, the coal is reduced to a dust-like, highly volatile state. The transferral of the cargo, together with the numerous wettings it receives, creates exactly the correct chemical conditions for spontaneous combustion. But, it should be stressed again that the fault, the blame, belongs with the men ashore who betray the ship and not with the ship itself. It is the owners and the underwriters, after all, who make the removal of the cargo necessary by allowing the ship to leave port in an unseaworthy condition.

The rewards and punishments which result from the *Judea*'s mishap are revealing. In this instance, since the *Judea*'s crew remain faithful to the dictates of the fellowship, since they serve the ship well, there is no sin to be atoned for and no breach of faith to be expiated. As a consequence, the crew escape unharmed and are successful in reaching shore, the destined and assigned end of all voyages. Moreover, as a kind of measure of the crew's innocence and as a token of both the ship's and the fellowship's approval of the crew's conduct, Marlow is permitted his intoxicating view of the enchanted East.

It should be observed that if the laws of Conrad's sea world seem, in some instances, oppressive or arbitrary or unfair, in the case of the *Judea,* at least, exact poetic justice is observed. The crew, innocent of all blame, not only come through their ordeal unharmed but they also bear the unspoken "well done" of the craft. On the other hand, those who serve the ship badly, the owners and insurance men ashore, are fittingly punished. Since the interest in the ship of the men on land is wholly materialistic, it is entirely appropriate that they should suffer the material loss of the ship and its cargo. As for a more significant form of punishment, the shipowners and the underwriters, like the crew of the *Patna* and like Massy, are simply not worth the trouble. They are, at the very best, no more than probationary members of the fellowship; indeed, in *The Mirror of the Sea,* Conrad specifically excludes them from full membership:

No seaman ever cherished a ship, even if she belonged to him, merely because of the profit she put in his pocket. No one, I think, ever did; for a ship-owner, even of the best, has always been outside the pale of that sentiment embracing in a feeling of intimate, equal fellowship the ship and the man, backing each other against the implacable, if sometimes dissembled, hostility of their world of waters. (p. 137)

This passage would also seem to effectively exclude the perfidious Massy, of *The End of the Tether,* not only from the fellowship of the craft but also from any right to the appellation "worthy seaman."

Central as the matter of fidelity is, however, much more goes into a definitive statement of the seaman's relationship with and attitude toward a ship. The ship makes its appeal on many grounds and at many levels of attraction and affection. Ultimately, what seems to happen is that the pattern of the most profound of human relationships is repeated. The relationship between men and ships begins with trust and ends in love.

Curiously enough, in view of the masculine and virile nature of the craft, the love which Conrad envisions between man and ship is not fraternal, not a bond between brothers or friends, but rather the love of a man for a woman. Lingard's evocation of his feelings for the brig *Lightning* comes immediately to mind. Lingard, it will be remembered, professes that, to him, his ship is "precious—like old love; always desirable—like a strange woman; always tender—like a mother; always faithful—like the favorite daughter of a man's heart" (*The Rescue,* p. 10). It is surely significant that Lingard finds analogues for his affection for his ship in the different manifestations of feminine love— romantic love, maternal love, and filial love. One can scarcely avoid conjuring up the ancient cliché which assigns feminine properties to a ship and prompts men to speak of a ship as "she" or "her." One can also scarcely avoid suggesting that the basis for feminizing a ship transcends her grace and beauty and her capacity for loyalty. The ship is a "she" because she is capable of engendering love in a man and is, in turn, the natural and proper recipient of this love.

The ship as an object of the seaman's deepest affection is to be found in many places in Conrad. We may return to Lingard and *The Rescue* for another statement of Lingard's affinity for the *Lightning:*

He had often heard men say that Tom Lingard cared for nothing on earth but for his brig—and in his thoughts he would smilingly correct the statement by adding that he cared for nothing *living* but the brig. (p. 10)

This is a lover speaking, and Lingard's profession is so phrased that he might just as readily be speaking of a woman as of a ship.

The profound nature of man's love for a ship is seen again

in *The Mirror of the Sea,* in a passage which reveals the commingling, in the seaman's mind, of trust and love:

A ship is not a slave. You must make her easy in a seaway, you must never forget that you owe her the fullest share of your thought, of your skill, of your self-love. If you remember that obligation, naturally and without effort, as if it were an instinctive feeling of your inner life, she will sail, stay, run for you as long as she is able, or, like a sea-bird going to rest upon the angry waves, she will lay out the heaviest gale that ever made you doubt living long enough to see another sunrise. (p. 56)

The obligations which Conrad places upon the seaman vis-à-vis his ship resemble nothing so much as a kind of nautical troth-plighting, and the dedication which this act of love engenders in the ship, in turn, is precisely the form of loyalty and self-effacement which has traditionally characterized the woman who is the object of love.

In another passage from *The Mirror of the Sea,* Conrad elevates men's love of ships to the highest possible plane. It is here, Conrad says, that we arrive at the best part of the whole seagoing adventure:

. . . the love of the sea, to which some men and nations confess so readily, is a complex sentiment wherein pride enters for much, necessity for not a little, and the love of ships—the untiring servants of our hopes and our self-esteem—for the best and most genuine part. (p. 136)

Finally, in yet another passage from *The Mirror of the Sea,* Conrad attempts to reach a definition of the seaman's love of ships, and, notably, the trait which seems to dominate is that which characterizes all true and genuine love, that is, its power to bring about a total sublimation of the self in the unreserved concern for the other:

The love that is given to ships is profoundly different from the love men feel for every other work of their hands—the love they bear to their houses, for instance—because it is untainted by the pride of possession. The pride of skill, the pride of responsibility, the pride of endurance there may be, but otherwise it is a disinterested sentiment. (pp. 136–37)

It appears, then, that by the very nature of things, all sailors feel an affinity and an affection for all ships, and it is an affinity and an affection of the highest order. But, there is a higher order of affection yet. This is the bond which individual seamen enjoy with individual ships, usually their own ships, and this bond truly passes all understanding. Lingard says as much to Mrs. Travers in *The Rescue:*

> "There's nothing in the world I love so much as this brig. . . . Nothing in the world. If I lost her I would have no standing room on the earth for my feet. You don't understand this. You can't."
>
> (p. 229)

Lingard's inability to communicate here is revealing, since he has found Mrs. Travers singularly perceptive and understanding on all other occasions.

Conrad, however, is not troubled by Lingard's loss of articulateness. Indeed, some of the most memorable passages in the sea tales are those in which he succeeds, as no other writer has, in vivifying this unique and elusive relationship, one man's love for a special ship.

As a first instance of the extraordinary power which a ship can exercise on a seaman, we may turn again to Tom Lingard in *The Rescue.* So close and so complete is the understanding between Lingard and the brig *Lightning,* that Lingard echoes the conventional plaint of lovers in speaking of his ship; he is lost without her, and absent from the *Lightning,* Lingard is incomplete:

> "Do you understand what I mean, Mrs. Travers? . . . They are afraid of me because I know how to fight this brig. They fear the brig because when I am on board her, the brig and I are one. An armed man—don't you see? Without the brig I am disarmed, without me she can't strike. So Daman thinks. He does not know everything but he is not far off the truth." ((pp. 226–27)

While there are no grounds to question Lingard's sincerity, at least in his own mind, he *is* something of a romantic and he has, perhaps, slightly overstated the case. In the three tales in which Lingard appears, there are several instances where he demonstrates considerable competence and self-sufficiency, with or without the brig.

Captain Whalley, in *The End of the Tether*, does not overstate the case when he says farewell to the *Fair Maid*. On his retirement, Whalley has bought the bark *Fair Maid*, with the professed intention of becoming something of a gentleman sailor. Actually, Whalley's real intent is to preserve some tie with the sea and, more important, with ships. When he suffers serious financial reverses, Whalley is forced to sell the bark. He takes leave of the *Fair Maid* in the following terms, and here there is no exaggeration. Whalley is, indeed, incomplete without his ship and horribly alone:

He knew that after this ship there would be no other; and the hopes of his youth, the exercise of his abilities, every feeling and achievement of his manhood, had been indissolubly connected with ships. He had served ships; he had owned ships; and even the years of his actual retirement from the sea had been made bearable by the idea that he had only to stretch out his hand full of money to get a ship. He had been at liberty to feel as though he were the owner of all the ships in the world. The selling of this one was weary work; but when she passed from him at last, when he signed the last receipt, it was as though all the ships had gone out of the world together, leaving him on the shore of inaccessible oceans. (p. 517)

In a very real sense, the *Fair Maid* is the last ship with which Whalley will have any meaningful relationship, and, in an equally real sense, it can be said that Whalley's career ends with the passing of the *Fair Maid*. There is still the *Sofala*, it is true; but for Whalley, the *Sofala* is less a ship and more a means to an end, and his three years aboard her are essentially an anticlimactic epilogue to his career.

Love at first sight is apparently possible between a man and a ship. This, at any rate, is what happens to the new captain in *The Shadow-Line* when he catches his initial glimpse of his command in the harbor at Bangkok:

At the first glance I saw that she was a high-class vessel, a harmonious creature in the lines of her fine body, in the proportioned tallness of her spars. Whatever her age and her history, she had preserved the stamp of her origin. She was one of those craft that in virtue of their design and complete finish will never look old. Amongst her companions moored to the bank, and all bigger than herself, she looked like a creature of high breed—an Arab steed in a string of cart-horses. (p. 49)

So rapt in his study of his ship is the captain that he scarcely hears the caustic comment of the master of the *Melita,* the ship which has brought him to Bangkok: "I hope you are satisfied with her, Captain" (p. 49). The young captain is more than satisfied. He goes on to contemplate the ship in the awed but delighted tones of a man who has just discovered that there is, in the world, a kindred soul whom he can love and cherish:

I did not even turn my head. It was the master of the steamer, and whatever he meant, whatever he thought of her, I knew that, like some rare women, she was one of those creatures whose mere existence is enough to awaken an unselfish delight. One feels that it is good to be in the world in which she has her being. (p. 49)

Rapture is, perhaps, reserved for the young, and so there is a certain reticence about Captain Allistoun's affection for his ship, the *Narcissus,* but the affection is nonetheless genuine. Allistoun has commanded the *Narcissus* since her commissioning, and, we are told: "He loved his ship, and drove her unmercifully; for his secret ambition was to make her accomplish some day a brilliantly quick passage which would be mentioned in nautical papers" (p. 318). Herein, there is no self-seeking on Allistoun's part but rather an honest zeal for the ship which he loves to appear in the best light. It is rather like the desire of the lover to have his loved one merit the approbation of his friends and associates. Mr. Burns, in *The Shadow-Line,* casts some light on Allistoun's motivation. "A ship," Mr. Burns observes, "needed . . . the chance to show the best she could do" (p. 56). In this context, Allistoun's eagerness for a record passage is wholly disinterested; it merely reflects his anxiety for the *Narcissus* "to show the best she could do."

The love of a ship can move even the most reserved and most stoic of men. Captain MacWhirr, of *Typhoon,* qualifies under both superlatives. He is scarcely a demonstrative man. He has, we are informed, "just enough imagination to carry him through each successive day, and no more" (p. 4). Yet, when at the height of the hurricane his ship is threatened with a real and present danger, MacWhirr retires to his cabin. Alone with his ship, he utters the words which are almost a supplication: "I wouldn't like to lose her" (p. 90). For MacWhirr, this is an

extraordinary emotional outburst, the equivalent of several passages of a lover's anguished despair at an impending separation.
And the outpouring is prompted by MacWhirr's very genuine,
though not overtly apparent, love for his ship.

The most interesting and most instructive study in Conrad
of the close bond between a man and a ship comes in *Heart of
Darkness*, in Charlie Marlow's account of his adventures with
the "battered, twisted, ruined, tin-pot" steamboat which he pilots
up the Congo. At the outset, Marlow feels nothing but a disdain,
bordering on contempt, for his extraordinary command. The
origin of this disdain is two-fold: first, Marlow's dignity, not to
mention his masculinity, has been bruised by the necessity of
compromising himself (so he sees it) in enlisting his aunt's help
in finding a post; second, "the dear enthusiastic soul" has aggravated the injury unwittingly by going on at length about
Marlow's prospects with the company and the role he might
play in the grand undertaking in the Congo. Thus, Marlow is
direly in need of some form of relief from his frustrations, and
the steamboat is a perfect scapegoat. It undoubtedly soothes
Marlow's injured ego to dismiss the steamboat as "a two-penny-
halfpenny river-steamboat with a penny whistle attached" (p. 12)
or as "that wretched, old, mangled steamboat" (p. 28); further,
Marlow's disdain is, in part, the natural hauteur of the seagoing
sailor for all manner of landlocked craft. It should be remembered that Marlow's last tour of duty comprised six years of
sailing fine ships throughout the exotic East. It is something
of a comedown to be reduced to a battered steamboat. And, the
force of the designation "boat" must not be overlooked. Marlow
(and Conrad) would make a clear distinction between oceangoing vessels, which are "ships," and smaller landlocked vessels,
which are called by the lesser term, "boats." With the exception
of submarines which are always referred to as "boats," the distinction is preserved in most navies today.

As a further insult to his already aggrieved sense of injury,
Marlow finds that his "wretched" command is not even navigable. It is, in fact, resting half-submerged in the river at the
Central Station with its bottom torn out. This is the nadir between man and ship. As Marlow says, "I asked myself what I

was to do there, now my boat was lost" (p. 21).

The bond that is ultimately formed between Marlow and the steamboat is all the more extraordinary in view of this un-promising beginning. Marlow himself admits, "I did not see the real significance of that wreck at once" (p. 21). In time, how-ever, understanding comes and Marlow is able to speak of the steamboat as an "influential friend" (p. 29), in other words, a friend who can do something for him. What the steamboat does for Marlow is to provide him with something real, something tangible, which serves as a shield to protect Marlow from the phantoms and the fears and the madness which beset him on all sides. Marlow's preoccupation with the steamboat also provides him with the restraint which is so important for survival in the Congo. (Further examples of restraint in *Heart of Darkness* which might be added to those cited earlier are the bookkeeper, who has bought his restraint at the price of his humanity, and the manager, whose unfailing good health provides his restraint.)

Marlow's commitment to something outside himself is a considerable step toward an affection which can grow into love. Indeed, with the passing of time, Marlow uses the very word in speaking of his growing bond with the steamboat: "She was nothing so solid in make, and rather less pretty in shape, but I had expended enough hard work on her to make me love her" (p. 29).

The degree of Marlow's commitment to his command may be seen in the forsaking-all-others gesture which he makes in devoting all his attention to the recovery of the steamboat: "I went to work the next day, turning, so to speak, my back on that station" (p. 23). And Marlow's dedication is reciprocated. The steamboat is always there for Marlow to call on, and call on it he does. When, for instance, Marlow has his lengthy conversa-tion with the brickmaker, the "papier-mâché Mephistopheles" (p. 26), as Marlow terms him, he has his shoulders firmly braced against the hull of the steamboat, and the symbolic action is not accidental. In this way, with his back against something solid for support, Marlow can face his enemies without the danger of being taken unaware, from the rear. They must attack, if they will, from the front, where he can see them. Again, when Marlow overhears the anxious exchange between the manager and his uncle, he does so "lying flat on the deck of my steamboat" (p. 31), with something real and tangible under him.

Marlow sums up his encounter with the steamboat in an exceptionally fine passage of Conradian prose, which is, at the same time, the best statement to be found in Conrad of the therapeutic value of work:

No, I don't like work. I had rather laze about and think of all the fine things that can be done. I don't like work—no man does—but I like what is in the work—the chance to find yourself. Your own reality—for yourself, not for others—what no other man can ever know. (p. 29)

Despite Marlow's frequent protestations of his defective spiritual vision, he has finally seen the "real significance" of the steamboat (p. 21). Stated quite simply, the steamboat has been nothing less than Marlow's salvation. It is Marlow's recognition of this immense indebtedness which brings him, all during the passage up river, to make the steamboat, once a target of his scorn, the object of his most meticulous care and concern, a care and concern born of gratitude, of admiration, of affection, even of love.

What we seem to have arrived at so far in this chapter is the proposition that all ships are created worthy, worthy of trust, worthy of love. But the proposition is not wholly accurate as stated, since, in Conrad's mind, some ships were created more worthy than others. The favored ones are the true birds of the sea, the sailing ships.

Conrad's predisposition for sailing ships is difficult to deny, but then, Conrad never denied it, nor did he attempt to hide it. His bias appears, in one form or another, explicitly or implicitly, in nearly all of his writings on the sea.

This partiality for sailing ships is a consequence of Conrad's own career and his own experiences at sea. Over and above the period devoted to the river steamboat that Conrad-Marlow piloted up the Congo, Conrad spent only ten months on steamboats, and two of these months he spent in port. Conrad's two decades at sea were essentially twenty years before the mast. In fact, as a seaman, Conrad was something of a transitional figure, going to sea during the declining but still rewarding days of sail and largely missing out on the coming mode of sea travel, the steamships, which were already beginning to dominate the sea lanes of the world.

Conrad was quite aware that his experience of the sea was thus limited, but he would have denied vehemently that he had "missed out." There is, for instance, the delightful ancedote in *A Personal Record* which reveals much about Conrad's attitude toward steamships. When the formalities of Conrad's examination for his master's ticket had been completed, the examiner, in an expansive moment, threw out to Conrad the observation: "You will go into steam presently. Everybody goes into steam" (p. 117). Conrad's reply reflects a certain wry humor at his own expense in the mock dismay he evidences. At the same time, there is not the slightest trace of regret that the examiner's prophecy did not come true:

There he was wrong. I never went into steam—not really. If I only live long enough I shall become a bizarre relic of a dead barbarism, a sort of monstrous antiquity, the only seaman of the dark ages who had never gone into steam—not really. (p. 117)

One need only catalogue the ships which appear in Conrad's sea stories to become aware of his marked predilection for sailing ships. The ships which serve best in Conrad's tales and which are most worthy of men's or a man's affection are all whitewinged birds of the sea—the *Narcissus,* the *Judea,* the *Fair Maid,* the *Lightning,* the two ships commanded by the new captains in *The Shadow-Line* and "The Secret Sharer," the brig *Flash* in *Almayer's Folly* and *An Outcast of the Islands.* In fact, Conrad wrote but one major story about a steamship, *Typhoon,* and even here the center of interest is the Captain, MacWhirr, rather than the ship, the *Nan-Shan.*

However, we do not have to rely on implicit evidence. Explicit evidence of Conrad's partiality toward sailing ships may be found in good measure in the memoir he wrote summing up the twenty years which he had devoted to the craft, *The Mirror of the Sea.* For example, when Conrad and his colleague in the fellowship, the elderly seaman, pause to admire the ships in the New South Dock, it is sailing ships on which their admiring gazes rest. Of these ships Conrad says: "It was a sight. The humblest craft that floats makes its appeal to a seaman by the faithfulness of her life; and this was the place where one beheld the aristocracy of ships" (p. 130). Earlier (p. 129), Conrad speaks of "cargo-carriers that would know no triumph but of speed in carrying a burden, no glory other than of a long service, no victory but that of an endless, obscure contest with the sea," and all that Conrad has said of a ship's capacity for loyalty, for fidelity, and for engendering the love of her masters comes into fine conjunction here. And it is significant, too, that the ships in the New South Dock make their appeal even in the most unfavorable light, that is, while still and lifeless at dock.

This same appeal is evident again, in *The Mirror of the Sea,* in Conrad's mental picture, a "perfect picture," of a sailing ship in harbor:

For a ship with her sails furled on her squared yards, and reflected from truck to water-line in the smooth gleaming sheet of a landlocked harbor, seems, indeed, to a seaman's eye the most perfect picture of slumbering repose. (p. 21)

And, a moment later, Conrad gives us this striking view of a ship arriving in port:

. . . this noisiness, this exultation at the moment of the ship's departure, make a tremendous contrast to the silent moments of her arrival in a foreign roadstead—the silent moments when, stripped of her sails, she forges ahead to her chosen berth, the loose canvas fluttering softly in the gear above the heads of the men standing still upon her decks. (p. 22)

But for Conrad, the appeal of the sailing ship goes far beyond her innate grace and beauty. The following passage from *The Mirror of the Sea,* a highly nostalgic evocation of a past that is no more, touches upon one of the special virtues, perhaps the unique virtue of the sailing ship—the bond which was once possible between men and ships, a bond which is now gone, having disappeared in the clatter of engines and the hiss of steam:

Here speaks the man of the masts and sails, to whom the sea is not a navigable element, but an intimate companion. The length of passages, the growing sense of solitude, the close dependence upon the very forces that, friendly to-day, without changing their nature, by the mere putting forth of their might, become dangerous to-morrow, make for that sense of fellowship which modern seamen, good men as they are, cannot hope to know. (pp.71–72)

(It is, perhaps, self-evident that "the man of the masts and sails" who purportedly speaks in this passage and Joseph Conrad are are not to be distinguished, the one from the other.)

All of which leads to the question, what, in Conrad's thinking, is wrong with steamships? Nothing very much—not really —and nothing fundamental. Conrad would stand by his position, enumerated earlier, that a steamship, like all ships, "is ever guiltless of the sins, transgressions, and follies of her men." Conrad can even joke about his own prejudice against steamships. There is, for instance, this playful passage in *The Shadow-Line*, in which the narrator speaks of the ship which, for no good reason, he suddenly gives up in Singapore:

. . . a most excellent Scottish ship—for she was that from the keel up—excellent sea-boat, easy to keep clean, most handy in every way, and if it had not been for her internal propulsion, worthy of any man's love. (p. 5)

And yet, there is something which, in Conrad's eyes, makes a steamship a lesser being.

For one thing, although Conrad might be uncomfortable with words like "romance," "adventure," "glamor," these are the very attributes which seem to have been lost to the seafarer's world with the advent of the steamship. Consider, for example, the disenchanted romantic, the narrator, who speaks in this passage from *An Outcast of the Islands*. He begins by conjuring up the sea of the past, and then there is a startling turn:

The sea, perhaps because of its saltness, roughens the outside but keeps sweet the kernel of its servants' soul. The old sea; the sea of many years ago, whose servants were devoted slaves and went from youth to age or to a sudden grave without needing to open the book of life, because they could look at eternity reflected on the element that gave the life and dealt the death. Like a beautiful and unscrupulous woman, the sea of the past was glorious in its smiles, irresistible in its anger, capricious, enticing, illogical, irresponsible; a thing to love, a thing to fear. It cast a spell, it gave joy, it lulled gently into boundless faith; then with quick and causeless anger it killed. But its cruelty was redeemed by the charm of its inscrutable mystery, by the immensity of its promise, by the supreme witchery of its possible favor. Strong men with childlike hearts were faithful to it, were content to live by its grace—to die by its will. That was the sea before the time when the French mind set the Egyptian muscle in motion and produced a dismal but profitable ditch. Then a great pall of smoke sent out by countless steamboats was spread over the restless mirror of the Infinite. The hand of the engineer tore down the veil of the terrible beauty in order that greedy and faithless landlubbers might pocket dividends. The mystery was destroyed. Like all mysteries, it lived only in the hearts of its worshippers. The hearts changed; the men changed. The once loving and devoted servants went out armed with fire and iron, and conquering the fear of their own hearts became a calculating crowd of cold and exacting masters. The sea of the past was an incomparably beautiful mistress, with inscrutable face, with cruel and promising eyes. The sea of to-day is a used-up drudge, wrinkled and defaced by the churned-up wakes of brutal propellers, robbed of the enslaving charm of its vastness, stripped of its beauty, of its mystery and of its promise. (pp. 12–13)

A sense of loss also pervades this passage from *The Mirror of the Sea,* and the passage itself hints strongly that modern-day seagoing is less art and more method and a terribly mechanized and formularized method at that:

The taking of a modern steamship about the world (though one would not minimize its responsibilities) has not the same quality of intimacy with nature, which, after all, is an indispensable condition to the building up of an art. It is less personal and a more exact calling; less arduous, but also less gratifying in the lack of close communion between the artist and the medium of his art. It is, in short, less a matter of love. (p. 30)

The mindless precision which Conrad envisions as being involved in taking a steamship to sea is perhaps best exemplified in *The End of the Tether.* Here is Conrad's description of a typical passage of the *Sofala,* and what chiefly emerges is a sense of the excessive monotony of the procedure and of Whalley's consequent acute boredom:

She could always be depended upon to make her courses. Her compasses were never out. She was no trouble at all to take about. . . . She made her landfalls to a degree of the bearing, and almost to a minute of her allowed time. At any moment, as he [Captain Whalley] sat on the bridge without looking up, or lay sleepless in his bed, simply by reckoning the days and the hours he could tell where he was—the precise spot of the beat. He knew it well, too, this monotonous huckster's round, up and down the Straits; he knew its order and its sights and its people. (p. 506)

And, in a later passage in *The End of the Tether,* Conrad employs a superb metaphor to express the humdrum nature of going to sea in a steamship. The reference is to the firm of Gardner, Patteson & Company, Whalley's former employers:

Their ships now had yellow funnels with black tops, and a time-table of appointed routes like a confounded service of tramways. The winds of December and June were all one to them. (p. 512)

Crucial as the loss of the poetry and the adventure of life at sea under sail is, the steamship has brought with it other and more concrete deficiencies. At several junctures, Conrad complains about the noise of the steamship. There is, for instance, this passage from *The Mirror of the Sea,* in which Conrad draws a deliberate contrast between the din of the modern steamship and the swift, silent grace of the sailing ship:

The modern steamship advances upon a still and overshadowed sea with a pulsating tremor of her frame, an occasional clang in her depths, as if she had an iron heart in her iron body; with a thudding rhythm in her progress and the regular beat of her propeller, heard afar in the night with an august and plodding sound as of the march of an inevitable future. But in a gale, the silent machinery of a sailing-ship would catch not only the power, but the wild and exulting voice of the world's soul. (p. 38)

The contrast between the noise of the steamship and the quiet of the sailing ship is enlarged upon in another passage from *The Mirror of the Sea:*

No doubt a fair amount of climbing up iron ladders can be achieved by an active man in a ship's engine-room, but I remember moments when even to my supple limbs and pride of nimbleness the sailing-ship's machinery seemed to reach up to the very stars.
    For machinery it is, doing its work in perfect silence and with a motionless grace, that seems to hide a capricious and not always

governable power, taking nothing away from the material stores of the earth. Not for it the unerring precision of steel moved by white steam and living by red fire and fed with black coal. (p. 37)

One final instance, from *Typhoon,* of Conrad's singling out noise as a determining characteristic of the steamship. Next to Mac-Whirr's indomitable resolve, or, if you will, his incredible pig-headedness, the chief impression one retains from a reading of *Typhoon* is the vividly realized noise of the ship, which, in its clattering and clanging, rivals even the ear-bursting roar of the hurricane. Three passages from *Typhoon* come immediately to mind. The first is Conrad's description of the second engineer at work in his domain below decks, and the atmosphere of the engine room has all the nerve-shattering decibel quality of an express subway train. The engineer, it will be seen, does not fail to make his contribution to the aural havoc:

"Blowing off all the time," went on yelling the second. With a sound as of a hundred scoured saucepans, the orifice of a ventilator spat upon his shoulder a sudden gush of salt water, and he volleyed a stream of curses upon all things on earth including his own soul, ripping and raving, and all the time attending to his business. With a sharp clash of metal the ardent pale glare of the fire opened upon his bullet head, showing his spluttering lips, his insolent face, and with another clang closed like the white-hot wink of an iron eye. (p. 71)

Second, there is the scene of the *Nan-Shan's* being loaded in dock. The passage has been quoted earlier in connection with the discussion of the influence of the land on ships, but it is worth repeating here as a fine rendering of the noise which, to Conrad, seems to be attendant on the daily activities of steamships. Jukes has just spoken and, we are told, his voice is heard

. . . above the harsh buzz of the *Nan-Shan's* friction winches. All of them were hard at work, snatching slings of cargo, high up, to the end of long derricks, only, as it seemed, to let them rip down recklessly by the run. The cargo chains groaned in the gins, clinked on coamings, rattled over the side. (p. 12)

Finally, there is another engine room scene in which machines and men seem to compete in creating cacophony:

The temperature in the engine-room had gone up to a hundred and seventeen degrees. Irritated voices were ascending through the skylight and through the fiddle of the stokehold in a harsh and resonant uproar, mingled with the angry clangs and scrapes of metal, as if men with limbs of iron and throats of bronze had been quarrelling down there. (p. 22)

Conrad also takes exception to certain none-too-subtle changes in the profession as a whole and in the status of the seaman in particular which the coming of steam has brought about. Some things, of course, remain the same—the enemy, the "inscrutable" sea, is still the same and the battlegrounds, the bridges and decks of ships, remain as before. But, there has been a significant change in the terms of the battle. No longer is it a manifestly unfair struggle pitting the seaman's cunning, resolution, sinew, nerves, and courage against a monstrous force. Steam has equalized the odds; it has given the seaman and the ship the capacity to meet power with power, and the battle has largely passed from the seaman's hands. The skill and the art of the craft may still be there, but they are seldom called upon. The seaman, as a result, is a diminished figure, virtually lost in the clash of brute force against brute force. There are two direct statements of this changing face of the arena of the sea in *The Mirror of the Sea,* and in each there is Conrad's reluctant acceptance of the new order of things coupled with a brief harking back to more dangerous, but more fulfilling days:

The efficiency of a steamship consists not so much in her courage as in the power she carries within herself. It beats and throbs like a pulsating heart within her iron ribs, and when it stops, the steamer, whose life is not so much a contest as the disdainful ignoring of the sea, sickens and dies upon the waves. The sailing-ship, with her unthrobbing body, seemed to lead mysteriously a sort of unearthly existence, bordering upon the magic of the invisible forces, sustained by the inspiration of life-giving and death-dealing winds. (pp. 63–64)

. . . your modern ship which is a steamship makes her passages on other principles than yielding to the weather and humoring the sea. She receives smashing blows, but she advances; it is a slogging fight, and not a scientific campaign. The machinery, the steel, the fire, the steam have stepped in between the man and the sea. (p. 72)

The notion of the steamship as a kind of blunt instrument with which the modern seaman forces his will on the sea is put forth on at least two occasions in *Typhoon*. MacWhirr has no use for Captain Wilson's "storm strategy" and sees no need to sail around the hurricane. He takes this position chiefly on the grounds that he is in command of "a full-powered steamship" which is capable of standing up to the storm and giving as good as it takes. In like fashion, in giving Jukes contingency instructions should he become a casualty of the storm, MacWhirr is quite explicit about the role of a "full-powered steamship" in a storm. It will be Jukes's duty to keep the ship "facing it—always facing it— that's the way to get through" (p. 89). MacWhirr envisions nothing less than a slugging match between two powerful forces, a naked show of strength, wherein the cunning of a man's right hand and his knowledge of the craft will play little part.

On the basis of the evidence considered in this chapter, Conrad's attitude toward ships and, since the equation is justified, his seamen's attitude, may be readily summed up. The issues involved are neither very complex nor very demanding. The ship is the natural and rightful repository of the seaman's trust. This trust, moreover, may be given with the confidence that it will never be violated. For, whatever man's "sins, transgressions, and follies," the ship remains faithful and guiltless. The ship is also the proper object of the seaman's affection and, even, love. Herein it rivals the other natural sources of affection—sweetheart, wife, home, family, friends. Finally, if the seaman concerned flourished during the days of sail, as did Joseph Conrad, then the sailing ship, as opposed to the steamship, will be the object of a special trust and affection.

CHAPTER FOUR

THE CRAFT

Most of the working truths on this earth are humble, not heroic. —*A Personal Record*

Those who read me know my conviction that the world, the temporal world, rests on a few very simple ideas; so simple that they must be as old as the hills. It rests notably, among others, on the idea of Fidelity. —*A Personal Record*

Fine sentiments be hanged! I had no time. I had to mess about with the white-lead and strips of woollen blankets helping to put bandages on those leaky steam-pipes. —*Heart of Darkness*

. . . in a sense, all sailors belong to one family; all are descended from that adventurous and shaggy ancestor who . . . accomplished the first coasting trip in a sheltered bay ringing with the admiring howls of his tribe. —*The Mirror of the Sea*

Two of Conrad's most knowledgeable and most enthusiastic critics, E. M. Forster and F. R. Leavis, have raised the same charge against him, namely, that he is very often given to needless obscurity. Forster, with his usual flair for the well-turned phrase, puts the matter this way in *Abinger Harvest* (New York, 1936, p. 138): "Is there not also a central obscurity, something noble, heroic, beautiful, inspiring half a dozen great books; but obscure, obscure? . . . he is misty in the middle as well as at the edges . . . the secret casket of his genius contains a vapor rather than a jewel." The formidable Dr. Leavis first quotes Forster and then adds the following stricture on his own behalf (*The Great Tradition*, New York, 1954, p. 219): "He is intent on making a virtue out of not knowing what he means. The vague and unrealizable, he asserts with strained impressiveness, is profoundly and tremendously significant."

One might question the proposition that Conrad doesn't know what he means. More accurately, it is often a case of Conrad's not saying what he means. And yet, painful as the admission is for any Conradian, it must be granted that both Forster's and Leavis's objections are justified. Conrad can, at times, be arcane, meaningless, and, most particularly, obscure. His pronouncements on the "craft" of the sea or, as he usually terms it, "the fellowship of the craft," constitute one of those times. Noticeably, Conrad engages in a good deal of rhetorical footwork and bobbing and weaving in talking about the "craft." For instance, Marlow, in *Lord Jim,* is allowed to run on at some length about "the little mysteries and the one great secret of the craft" (p. 28) and about the craft "whose whole secret could be expressed in one short sentence" (p. 27). So too in "Youth," Marlow speaks with much sincerity, no doubt, but with little clarity of "the strong bond of the sea, and also the fellowship of the craft" (p. 115). And, in *The Mirror of the Sea,* we hear Conrad speaking in his own voice, in conjunction with his meeting with the elderly seaman, of their joint "fellowship in the craft and mystery of the sea" (p. 131).

All this is very well, all very "noble, heroic, beautiful, inspiring," but one must agree with Forster that there is a "central obscurity," and perhaps with Leavis that these words seem to touch upon the "vague and unrealizable." What *is* the "secret" of the craft which Conrad-Marlow threatens to reduce to one sentence and what *are* the "mysteries" which are conjured up so enigmatically?

Conrad might have done well to pay heed to his spokesman, Marlow, for Marlow is right in believing that the whole secret of the craft "could be expressed in one short sentence." In fact, Conrad has written that sentence in *The Mirror of the Sea:* "After all, the only mission of a seaman's calling is to keep ships' keels off the ground" (p. 67). This is the sum and all of the secret of the craft and is, moreover, the very raison d'être of the craft. Marlow similarly reduces the matter to its simplest terms, although somewhat more imaginatively, in *Heart of Darkness:* "For a seaman, to scrape the bottom of the thing that's supposed to float all the time under his care is the unpardonable sin" (p. 35).

Having exposed the "secret" of the craft, may we now hope to throw some light on its "mysteries"? I am sure we can; Conrad has again been needlessly vague. The mysteries of the craft appear to be those guiding principles, those rules of conduct which all worthy seamen must subscribe to and adhere to in order to carry out the basic mission of keeping the ship afloat. These rules for success and salvation at sea are three-fold: the seaman must never lose sight of the trust placed in him in having the ship committed to his care; he must be willing to work diligently and devotedly to the end of keeping his ship safe; he must be aware of his place in the long continuum of the craft, aware of its traditions, and aware of those who have come before him who were worthy and of those who come after him and will be worthy.

Conrad's two autobiographical memoirs, *A Personal Record* and *The Mirror of the Sea*, both treat at some length of his years as a seaman, the years of his active membership in the fellowship. In each of these accounts, the term "fidelity" or its variant, "trust," appears with such frequency that fidelity looms as the distinguishing and defining virtue of the seaman's life and appears to be the dominant impression which Conrad retained from his career before the mast. These assumptions are not unfounded; from the evidence of Conrad's works, fidelity is precisely the attribute of life at sea which he would single out and convey to his reader.

There is, for instance, the passage already quoted from *The Mirror of the Sea* in which Conrad identifies fidelity as the central working virtue of the seagoing world:

. . . not, indeed, that I mean to say that ships are unruly; on the contrary, they are faithful creatures, as so many men can testify. And faithfulness is a great restraint, the strongest bond laid upon the self-will of men and ships on this globe of land and sea. (pp. 110–11)

And, again, in *The Mirror of the Sea*, Conrad concludes his passage on the seaman's basic mission, keeping his ship afloat, by making clear that this commitment goes beyond the purely practical and beyond the realm of duty. It is, in fact, a "trust"

To keep ships afloat is his business; it is his trust; it is the effectiv
formula at the bottom of all these vague impulses, dreams, and illu
sions that go to the making up of a boy's vocation. (p. 67)

But the major statement of the role of fidelity in the fellow
ship of the craft comes in *A Personal Record*. Conrad is seldom
so positive and so firm in his conviction as he is in the two
sentences which serve as an epigraph to this chapter:

Those who read me know my conviction that the world, the tem
poral world, rests on a few very simple ideas; so simple that they
must be as old as the hills. It rests notably, among others, on the
idea of Fidelity. (p. xxi)

Herein, fidelity assumes the proportions of the first and the fina
word, not only at sea, but in all of men's pursuits. Fidelity be
comes, in effect, the key with which to unlock the world entire.
In another passage from *A Personal Record*, Conrad re
affirms his conviction that fidelity is the be-all and end-all: "I
will make bold to say that neither at sea nor ashore have I ever
lost the sense of responsibility" (p. 111). We should not be put
off by Conrad's substitution of "responsibility" for "fidelity."
In Conrad's mind, the distinction between the two terms was not
large.

Finally, in *A Personal Record*, there occurs what might
be called the Conradian credo, on which, one senses, Conrad
would be willing to stand and be judged: "I do not know whether
I have been a good seaman, but I know I have been a very faithful one" (p. 110). What is chiefly to be noted here is the relative
emphasis given by the structure of the sentence to the good seaman and the faithful seaman. Matters of technical competence
and all manner of unspecified virtues seem to give way to the
single demand of fidelity, and the clear implication is that it is
better to be a faithful seaman than an accomplished seaman.

The same emphasis on fidelity may be seen in the sea tales.
In fact, when compiling a list of Conrad's stories of the sea, it
comes as something of a revelation to recognize that each is
concerned, in greater or lesser detail, with fidelity. In every one

of the sea tales, without exception, the theme of trust appears
as a major or a subsidiary issue, and each story treats of seamen,
either major or minor characters, who keep faith or who break
faith. It will be convenient to consider these instances of good
or bad faith in the sea tales in order of ascending importance.
We begin with minor characters whose fidelity is, of course, admirable, but is of lesser consequence in the story, and move
toward major characters whose fidelity, or lack of it, *is* the story.

Among the minor characters in the sea tales who keep faith
is the native fireman, in *Heart of Darkness,* who serves aboard
the steamboat during its passage up-river. Marlow tells us, with
fine irony, that he is "an improved specimen" (p. 37). He has
reached this august state because he has been taught to fire up
the steamboat's antiquated boiler and to keep the hands of the
pressure gauges within certain limits. He has also been taught
that should he neglect his duty "the evil spirit inside the boiler
would get angry through the greatness of his thirst, and take a
terrible vengeance" (pp. 37–38). The fireman, with the aid
of an "impromptu charm," performs his duties faithfully,
even during the hullabaloo going on over his head when the
steamboat is attacked. It might be argued, of course, that the
real source of the fireman's diligence is his fear of the consequences should he prove derelict. It might also be argued, however, that all men who keep faith are motivated, to some extent,
by the threat of sanctions. The French lieutenant in *Lord Jim,*
for example, remains aboard the abandoned *Patna* for thirty
hours, even though he believes that she might sink at any moment, largely because he fears the loss of honor. Physical fear,
the chief fear of the fireman, has been conquered by the lieutenant, or, at least, he has learned to live with it—"habit—
habit—necessity—do you see?—the eye of others—*voilà.* One
puts up with it" (p. 90). The level of fidelity would thus seem
to be in proportion to the level of the sanctions which apply.
By these terms, the French lieutenant is at a fairly high level,
since he is governed by an intangible, honor, while the native
is at a lower level, since in his case the sanctions (the threat of
the boiler) are more direct and immediate, more visible, so to
speak.

Similarly, in the case of the Malayan helmsman in *Lord Jim*

who remains aboard the *Patna* while her white crew abandoi
the ship, the sanctions which may be applied are quite visible
punishment lies in the hands of the white men. At the sam
time, a source of trust, of confidence, is equally visible to th
Malayan in the persons of the white men. He trusts them ab
solutely, and, even at the time of the inquiry, his faith remain
unshaken and he refuses to believe that the white men acter
out of such a simple motive as fear. Again, the fidelity evidence
here is at a lesser level, since it is easier to respond to a concret
and visible embodiment of trust and of the threat of sanction
than to maintain a commitment to some abstract concept
whether it be honor or the code of the fellowship of the craft

The captain, in *The Shadow-Line*, is bolstered in his desir
to keep faith by the added incentive of saving his ship and, eve
more important, of proving worthy of his first command. Yet
he acts chiefly from promptings which have no tangible form
which hardly even take form in his mind, much less on his lips
They all have to do, however, with the basic mission and th
basic trust of the fellowship, keeping his ship afloat. In th
captain's case, the sanctions are not immediate; they are no
present and not visible, and still the captain never swerves fror
his resolve to fulfill his trust. When the ship arrives in port, th
doctor who responds to the captain's signal for medical assist
ance is genuinely astonished at the feat of endurance and o
single-mindedness which the captain has accomplished. He ha
been on deck for seventeen days and has virtually brought th
ship to port unassisted. However, the captain's own remembranc
of the last night of the ordeal, when he is alone all night at th
wheel, has no touch of heroics but, rather, a dogged, selfles
determination to keep faith:

And I steered, too tired for anxiety, too tired for connecte
thought. I had moments of grim exultation and then my hear
would sink awfully at the thought of that forecastle at the other en
of the dark deck, full of fever-stricken men—some of them dying
By my fault. But never mind. Remorse must wait, I had to stee
(pp.125–26)

But fidelity does not *require* heroics in the sea tales to fin
proper expression. Conrad gets some of his best effects throug

understatement. For example, as the *Narcissus* makes its way on the long passage from Bombay to London, the threat of heavy weather becomes imminent. Captain Allistoun, as is proper for the man who bears the final responsibility, meets the threat on the bridge. The steward, working forward with great difficulty, attempts to bring Allistoun a cup of hot coffee "half of which the gale blew out of the cup before it reached the master's lips" (p. 336). Then, there is this splendid passage with its studiously underplayed ending:

He drank what was left gravely in one long gulp, while heavy sprays pattered loudly on his oilskin coat, the seas swishing broke about his high boots; and he never took his eyes off the ship. (p. 336)

So, too, the old sailor Jörgenson, in *The Rescue,* eschews heroics but still manages to say much in a few words. Jörgenson, as Conrad puts it, has been "called back into the life of men" (p. 115) by being placed in charge of the battered schooner *Emma* which Lingard has deliberately run aground near Belarab's settlement on the Shore of Refuge. The *Emma* contains all of Lingard's supplies of arms and ammunition and is more a stationary fort than a ship. Yet, Jörgenson's sense of fidelity to his command, even though it is a beached command and no longer capable of putting to sea, is unchanged. In the course of a letter, in which he brings Lingard up to date on what has been happening on the Shore of Refuge, Jörgenson, with his usual taciturnity, touches upon the matter of fidelity and his one sentence speaks volumes: "All you are worth in this world, Tom, is here in the *Emma,* under my feet, and I would not leave my charge even for half a day" (p. 172). (It can be said, in passing, that part of Jim's trouble, as diagnosed by Marlow, is his expectation that life at sea will be on the heroic scale and in accordance with the "course of light holiday literature" [*Lord Jim*, p. 4] which he read as a boy. Conrad is making clear, in *The Rescue* and elsewhere, that most of the world's heroics are muted and subdued and played in low key.)

This same unheroic, self-effacing fidelity and uncomplicated sense of commitment may be seen in Mr. Baker, the chief mate of the *Narcissus.* Baker does enjoy the advantage of having a fine example of faithfulness, Captain Allistoun, before him, but at the same time it is clear that Baker's dedication is such that it scarcely requires the added spur of admiration and emulation. Conrad refers, in fact, to Baker as "a model chief mate" (p. 447). And indeed he is, and never more so than when the crew, having brought the ship through the worst of the storm and having rescued Jimmy Wait from almost certain drowning, begin to feel a bit satisfied with themselves. They now feel competent to pass judgment on Allistoun's decision not to cut the masts and they decide that the captain doesn't "care" for them. It falls to Baker to bring the crew back into line, and he does so in a manner which leaves no doubt that Baker's concept of the sea-man's obligation to keep his ship safe is without restrictions or limitations: "Care for you! . . . Why should he care for you? Are you a lot of women passengers to be taken care of? We are here to take care of the ship—and some of you ain't up to that" (p. 364). Baker as practicing psychologist deserves comment. Surely, nothing could be more rankling to a group of able-bodied seamen than to be dismissed as "a lot of women" and, to add harm to injury, to be denied their identity and characterized as mere passengers aboard a ship.

Conrad's position on the unheroic nature of life at sea not-withstanding, there *are* instances of keeping faith in the sea stories which rise to the level of the heroic, although not to the theatrical heights which Jim envisions. Leggatt, in "The Secret Sharer," for instance, risks everything, his career and indeed his life, for the sake of keeping his ship afloat. His accidental strangling of the rebellious crewman condemns him under civil and moral law, but in terms of the discipline of the sea Leggatt has committed an even graver offense. He arrogates the lawful authority of the master of the ship, for it is Leggatt and not Archbold who gives the command to set a reefed foresail. The irony is that the very act which condemns Leggatt is the salvation of the ship, and even Archbold admits that Leggatt's timely order saved the ship. But this does not signify. Leggatt's is a capital offense under the civil and moral codes and under the special code of the sea. Given the stakes involved, Leggatt's action falls into the category of the heroic, but his only attempt at justification is characterized by the same unassuming, unheroic tone seen earlier in Jörgenson's letter: "I was," says Leggatt, "an officer of that old coal-wagon, anyhow—" (p. 681), and as such, he does what he must do to keep his ship afloat.

There is certainly something of the heroic in "Youth" in the elderly Beard's obsession with keeping his ship alive and getting her safely to Bangkok. Beard's obsession is of such proportions, in fact, that it must be seen as either heroic or verging on madness. Marlow provides the clue as to how we should respond. When the ship is nearly blown in two by the explosion of the coal gas, Beard's first concern is to restore the ship's routine and to get her back on course. Marlow reports, in awestruck tones:

And, mark, he noticed directly the wheel deserted and his bark off her course—and his only thought was to get that miserable, stripped, undecked, smoldering shell of a ship back again with her head pointing at her port of destination. Bangkok! That's what he was after. I tell you this quiet, bowed, bandy-legged, almost deformed little man was immense in the singleness of his idea. (p. 136)

Even when it is evident that the *Judea*'s wounds are mortal, when Beard is, at best, commanding the ruined skeleton of a ship, he insists on keeping faith. He refuses the assistance of the passing steamer *Somerville:* "Thank you! No! . . . We must see the last of the ship" (p. 141). And when the time comes to leave the *Judea,* such is Beard's sense of the trust he bears that he insists on saving as much gear as possible "for the underwriters" (p. 142). Beard may have lost a ship, but he has lost it in good order and he will carry with him to Bangkok the tokens of his fidelity.

Singleton's thirty-hour vigil at the wheel of the *Narcissus* can hardly be spoken of without resorting to some such terms as "heroic" or even "epic." Indeed, Conrad's handling of the episode is sufficient evidence that he himself is aware of dealing with something extraordinary. His account of Singleton at the helm comes at the end of one of the sections of the novel, and it is placed there for added emphasis. Then too, just prior to the Singleton episode, Conrad has been describing, in considerable detail, the frantic efforts of the crew to right the ship. The pages of the novel have been filled with the tumult of the storm scene,

the sheer noise of the activity on deck, the shouts and curses of
the men and the steady roar of the great wind. There is a striking
change of pace as Conrad turns his attention to Singleton, isolated and alone at the wheel. It is almost as if Conrad, like the
Narcissus's complement, had forgotten about Singleton. From
the clamor and excitement and uproar of the deck, we move to
the serene, almost stately, picture of Singleton at the wheel:

Apart, far aft, and alone by the helm, old Singleton had deliberately
tucked his white beard under the top button of his glistening coat.
Swaying upon the din and tumult of the seas, with the whole battered length of the ship launched forward in a rolling rush before his
steady old eyes, he stood rigidly still, forgotten by all, and with an
attentive face. In front of his erect figure only the two arms moved
crosswise with a swift and sudden readiness, to check or urge again
the rapid stir of circling spokes. (p. 373)

To conclude this passage, Conrad bestows upon Singleton the
highest possible accolade, an accolade which gains emphasis
through another instance of deliberate understatement. Conrad
says of Singleton: "He steered with care" (p. 373).
    A really extraordinary instance of fidelity carried to the
uttermost limits is the case, in *Lord Jim,* of Montagu Brierly,
"Big Brierly," master of the crack ship *Ossa* of the Blue Star
Line. Brierly, a member of the Board of Inquiry convened to
look into the *Patna* affair, is vehement in his condemnation of
Jim—"let him creep twenty feet underground and stay there!"
(p. 41). Marlow is shocked by the extent of Brierly's outrage,
especially since Brierly gives every appearance of being thoroughly bored with the whole affair. The basis for Brierly's ani-
mosity is that Jim has not kept faith, that he has violated his
trust and has compromised the fellowship of the craft. Brierly
delivers what is perhaps the best statement in all of Conrad of
the commonality of the bond of sworn trust which unites all
worthy seamen. He observes to Marlow:

"We are trusted. Do you understand?—trusted! Frankly, I don't
care a snap for all the pilgrims that ever came out of Asia, but a
decent man would not have behaved like this to a full cargo of old
rags in bales. We aren't an organized body of men, and the only

thing that holds us together is just the name for that kind of decency. Such an affair destroys one's confidence." (p. 42)

Shortly after delivering this pronouncement, Brierly commits suicide by jumping over the side of his ship while at sea. Later, in pondering the case, Marlow provides us with the key to Brierly's exceptional behavior. "At bottom," says Marlow, "poor Brierly must have been thinking of himself" (p. 41). Brierly's apparent boredom while sitting in judgment on Jim is a pose which he maintains only with considerable difficulty. In actual fact, Brierly is quite alert; he has suddenly had opened up to him a new and terrifying vista. Brierly, an essentially honest man, recognizes himself in Jim—Jim is, after all, "one of us." Brierly is forced to consider the possibility that "Big Brierly," winner of a "gold chronometer" and "a pair of binoculars with a suitable inscription" (p. 35) for his bravery at sea, might fail, given the right set of circumstances, just as Jim has failed. He is forced to face an even more unacceptable prospect, that of spending his life as something less than the master of the crack ship *Ossa* should he fail. Whether personal vanity or sincere dedication is the governing factor (and I would opt for the latter), Montagu Brierly finds the stakes too high and chooses his singularly dramatic way of ending the game. Brierly's dedication is attested to in that, before he goes over the rail, he gives his chief mate, Jones, the course corrections to be made during the next watch, sets the taff-rail log and puts a drop of oil in it. Brierly, in other words, leaves his command shipshape.

This is the proper place to take cognizance of the fact that there are two suicides among Conrad's seamen. In addition to Brierly, Captain Whalley of the *Sofala* takes his own life. Conrad's attitude toward these two acts of self-destruction is rather difficult to come at. Despite his nominal Catholicism, he does not seem to invoke moral sanctions; perhaps his own abortive attempt at suicide gave Conrad a special insight into how one reaches the state of mind where suicide appears to be the only solution. And yet, Brierly's and Whalley's suicides *are* moral issues under the code of the fellowship of the craft, and I submit that Conrad would distinguish between the two cases. In the light of the code, Whalley's suicide is a failure. In fact, it is with the very act of taking his life that Whalley violates his trust and breaks faith. In choosing to go down with the *Sofala*, Whalley allows his ship to be sunk, and, even more important, he carries the evidence of Massy's crime with him. Brierly, on the other hand, in plunging into the sea preserves the code and keeps faith by this very act and in the most uncompromising manner.

Grand as Brierly's gesture is, however, he is a troubled man, who, *in extremis,* chooses not to risk. Captain MacWhirr of the *Nan-Shan,* Conrad's prime example of the faithful seaman, blithely accepts any risk and faces up to everything that the sea, the elements, the chances of the day, or the destiny of the years can throw at him. Except for his one brief moment of uncertainty —"I wouldn't like to lose her"—he braves all and remains unshaken in his constancy and in his resolve. MacWhirr's appraisal of the situation as the storm approaches is simplicity itself, unalloyed by doubt: "All we've got to do is to take them [the Chinese coolies] to Fu-chau, being timed to get there before noon on Friday. If the weather delays me—very well" (p. 34). And when the matter of adopting "storm strategy" and steering a course to avoid the gale comes up, MacWhirr is equally clearsighted and equally fixed in his resolve:

> "But suppose I went swinging off my course and came in two days late, and they asked me: 'Where have you been all that time, Captain?' What could I say to that? 'Went around to dodge the bad weather,' I would say. 'It must've been dam' bad,' they would say. 'Don't know,' I would have to say; 'I've dodged clear of it.' " (p. 34)

MacWhirr has sometimes been taken to task by critics for his bullheadedness in insisting on keeping his ship headed into the storm, but it must be conceded that his logic is impeccable. What, indeed, would he say, having spent two days dodging a storm he hasn't seen and which he cannot swear did, in fact, exist. Then too, it must be remembered that MacWhirr is in command of a full-powered steamship."

Throughout the *Nan-Shan*'s passage through the typhoon, MacWhirr never loses sight of his primary mission—to keep his ship afloat and to bring her safely into port. This is his part of the compact he has made with the *Nan-Shan* and he proposes to fulfill it, just as he has full confidence that the ship will prove faithful, too. MacWhirr observes to Jukes, for instance, "We must trust her to go through it and come out on the other side"; the key word here is "trust." The extent of MacWhirr's commitment to his ship is best evidenced in a passage which comes after he has learned of the disorder which has broken out among the coolies in the 'tween-deck and has dispatched Jukes to deal with it. There follows this revealing glimpse into MacWhirr's thinking: "If the ship had to go after all, then, at least, she wouldn't be going to the bottom with a lot of people in her fighting teeth and claw. That would have been odious" (p. 85). In other words, if the *Nan-Shan* must sink, she will go decently and in good order, her captain in command, having fulfilled all the dictates of the code of the craft and having done all that could be done for his ship. MacWhirr is rewarded for his fidelity. He is spared the "annoyance," as Conrad puts it in almost comic understatement, of losing his ship and is permitted to bring her safely into port at Fu-chau.

But this is no more than what MacWhirr intends, even expects, to do. There is, as we have observed earlier, a noticeable imbalance in the system of rewards and punishments which prevails in Conrad's sea world. The men who keep faith are generally acknowledged with little more than a word of approval from their admirer, Joseph Conrad, while those who break faith are often punished in the extreme, being visited by a retribution that is swift and, on occasion, cataclysmic. We might consider a few cases of breaches of fidelity in the sea tales, again moving from lesser to greater instances, and, at the same time, devote some attention to the matter of how each of the malefactors is punished.

The defection of the helmsman in *Heart of Darkness*, for instance, is at a lower level of importance for the purposes of the story. Although his dereliction and subsequent death are sources of annoyance to Marlow, since they combine to confine him to the wheel of the steamboat, the fate of the helmsman does not really change the texture of the story or blur the focus which is firmly fixed on Charlie Marlow. The punishment which meets the helmsman, however, is unexpected. It would appear to be, in fact, a case of the punishment greatly exceeding the crime. At the same time, it can be argued that during the few seconds that it takes the helmsman to fire the rifle out of the pilot house window, the steamboat is placed in the gravest peril. It should be kept in mind that the steamboat is not on the open sea where there is room for maneuvering or even time to rectify an error in judgment by the humans into whose hands the ship has been placed. Marlow renders very vividly the nice problem in navigation which the river presents with its hidden banks and sunken stones and endless snags: "Imagine a blindfolded man set to drive a van over a bad road. I sweated and shivered over that business considerably, I can tell you" (p. 35). Under these conditions, a lapse of only a few seconds is enough to, in Marlow's graphic phrasing, rip "the life out of the tin-pot steamboat" (p. 34). Under these conditions, the helmsman's transgression becomes a capital offense for which the proper punishment is assigned and extracted.

The point becomes clearer if we turn to another faithless helmsman, the helmsman in *The Nigger of the "Narcissus,"* presumably Singleton's relief and a feeble copy of the ancient mariner. As is true in *Heart of Darkness,* this helmsman's lapse, too, is no more than a minor episode and it has no significant bearing on the course of the story. The dereliction occurs when the half-hearted attempt at mutiny breaks out on the deck, culminating in Donkin's throwing the belaying pin in Allistoun's general direction. (Characteristically, Donkin can do nothing right.) The helmsman's curiosity is aroused by the hubbub. He leaves the wheel in order to make his way to a better vantage point. The *Narcissus,* of course, responds immediately and Conrad describes the action in a passage which concentrates on two issues: that any breach of trust has an immediate effect on the well-being of the ship; that the ship, faithful always to her part of the bargain, expects the same fidelity in return, a point which Conrad makes explicit in the closing sentence of the passage:

The *Narcissus,* left to herself, came up gently to the wind without anyone being aware of it. She gave a slight roll, and the sleeping sails woke suddenly, coming all together with a mighty flap against

the masts, then filled again one after another in a quick succession
of loud reports that ran down the lofty spars, till the collapsed main-
sail flew out last with a violent jerk. The ship trembled from trucks
to keel; the sails kept on rattling like a discharge of musketry; the
chain sheets and loose shackles jingled aloft in a thin peal; the gin
blocks groaned. It was as if an invisible hand had given the ship an
angry shake to recall the men that peopled her decks to the sense of
reality, vigilance, and duty. (p. 406)

The chief difference between the case of the steamboat and the
Narcissus is that, with the oceangoing ship, there is some margin
for error. There is even time for the ship to give a warning; the
wheel is manned again; the watch returns to duty, and no harm
is done. In fact, the helmsman's lapse has its positive effect. It
is the sudden danger in which the ship is placed that breaks the
restive mood of the crew and brings them back to the reality of
their situation. The helmsman, consequently, escapes with a
tongue lashing, presumably, and presumably from Mr. Baker,
who has little patience with such waywardness. In the final
analysis, the case of the *Narcissus*'s helmsman accommodates
itself better to our conventional notions of crime and punishment.

Captain Whalley's offense, however, is no minor affair; it is
central to *The End of the Tether*. Indeed, the story hinges on
Whalley's action and the tale is shaped toward the culminating
point when Whalley reaches the end of his tether and must
choose between love and honor. But, when we turn to the matter
of Whalley's punishment, we seem to have the obverse of the
case of the helmsman in *Heart of Darkness*. Whalley's crime
would seem to greatly exceed his punishment. On first reading,
in fact, it would appear that his transgression serves his ends
admirably. With the evidence of Massy's treachery safely in
Whalley's pockets at the bottom of the sea, the insurance company will have no course but to pay the claim, including the
£500 which will devolve on Whalley's daughter, Ivy. Thus, it
would appear, Whalley is home free. I would propose, however,
that the awareness of his offense, even for only the brief space
that it takes the *Sofala* to go under, is sufficient punishment for
a man of Whalley's probity. After all, it is egregious, indeed, for
the discoverer of "Whalley Passage" and a member in very good

standing of the fellowship of the craft to carry with him, as he leaves the world, the knowledge that he has betrayed a ship.

The most grievous case of breaking faith in the sea tales is, of course, Jim. Jim's failure, or inability, to fulfill a trust lies at the very heart of *Lord Jim* and gives the novel its special atmosphere and its bite. The fiasco aboard the *Patna* has been discussed at such length, evaluated and adjudged in so many ways and by so many critics, that it will be a positive act of good faith and good fellowship to spare the reader further speculation. Besides, such a discussion is digressive here, since we are not concerned with the motives for Jim's action, a complex matter highly disputed; we are concerned, rather, with his transgression against the code of the craft, a simple fact not disputed. For his transgression, Jim is adequately punished, not so much by his death as by the exquisite torture to which he puts himself in his belief that he has fallen short of what Conrad calls, in "The Secret Sharer," "that ideal conception of one's own personality every man sets up for himself secretly" (p. 651).

What does warrant some probing and analysis is a point which has not been sufficiently noted. In essence, Jim is subject to two codes, the code of the craft, and a highly personal code of his own devising which has to do with his romantic vision of himself as "a man destined to shine in the midst of dangers" (p. 5). It is to this latter code that Jim apparently feels any allegiance. He insists, for instance, on looking upon the *Patna* debacle as a "chance missed." Marlow's concern, on the other hand, is chiefly for the sanctity of the craft and, since he has insisted on Jim's right to membership ("He is one of us"), Marlow is angered by Jim's violation of the trust. Worse yet is Jim's fecklessness in being unaware of his failing, and this infuriates Marlow. "The real significance of crime," says Marlow, "is in its being a breach of faith with the community of mankind" (p. 95); and of his crime against this community of the sea, Jim seems to have little conception. Marlow sounds this note—the breach of communal faith—again in attempting to account to his auditors for his exasperation at Jim's insouciance:

"Don't you see what I mean by the solidarity of the craft? I was aggrieved against him, as though he had cheated me—me!—of a splendid opportunity to keep up the illusion of my beginnings, as though he had robbed our common life of the last spark of its glamor." (p. 80)

Jim's failure to measure up is aggravated by the fact that he promised so much and failed so spectacularly. Jim has all the right credentials: he comes from a good family in Essex; he is a "Conway" boy (I assume that Jim's apprentice days are spent aboard Conrad's favorite training ship, the alma mater of the Director of Companies in "Youth" and of both Leggatt and the captain in "The Secret Sharer"); he is physically attractive and looks the role of the most solid member of the fellowship. Jim's air of belonging is attested to by Marlow, who, over the years, has acquired a practiced eye on this score:

"I liked his appearance; I knew his appearance; he came from the right place; he was one of us. . . . He was the kind of fellow you would, on the strength of his looks, leave in charge of the deck—figuratively and professionally speaking. I say I would, and I ought to know. Haven't I turned out youngsters enough in my time, for the service of the Red Rag, to the craft of the sea . . .!" (p. 27)

It is thus doubly galling for Marlow that the appearance and the reality are so disparate. Marlow's exasperation at the betrayal which goes unrepented and, at the same time, his sense of loss at the promise which goes unfulfilled come through in this outburst which he directs at the select group of friends to whom he tells Jim's story:

"I tell you I ought to know the right kind of looks. I would have trusted the deck to that youngster on the strength of a single glance, and gone to sleep with both eyes—and, by Jove!—it wouldn't have been safe. There are depths of horror in that thought. He looked as genuine as a new sovereign, but there was some infernal alloy in his metal." (p. 28)

It is time to take stock. Applying the principle of ascending order of importance (for the story itself) to the various examples of fidelity and infidelity in the sea tales, we have arrived at Captain MacWhirr of the *Nan-Shan* as the Conradian seaman who enjoys the greatest measure of success in keeping the faith. Con-

versely, we must assign to Jim the doubtful distinction of failing
to keep faith most significantly and most spectacularly.

It is not by accident that we have come to these two men and
to this antithesis. Although the two tales, *Typhoon* and *Lord Jim*,
were separated by almost two years, it seems clear that Conrad
held Jim in his mind even as he brought MacWhirr to life.
The two seamen are closely related, in a complementary fashion;
MacWhirr and Jim represent, respectively, studies of the static
imagination on the one hand and the hyperactive imagination on
the other.

Conrad, it will be recalled from a passage quoted earlier,
characterized MacWhirr as "having just enough imagination to
carry him through each successive day, and no more" (*Typhoon,*
p. 4). And, observing the dictum which he put forth in the
"Preface" to *The Nigger of the "Narcissus"* that the artist's
task is to make us "see," Conrad permits, almost forces, the
reader to "see" MacWhirr's deficient imagination at work. For
instance, MacWhirr is simply unable to make the modest imaginative effort it would take to allow him to accept Jukes's affec-
tionate description of the *Nan-Shan*—"the old girl was as good as
she was pretty" (p. 7). "It would never have occurred to Captain
MacWhirr," we are told, "to express his favorable opinion so
loud or in terms so fanciful" (p. 7). To the literal-minded Mac-
Whirr, there would have been something almost sacrilegious in
taking such liberties with "a full-powered steamship." In the
same vein, it has also never occurred to MacWhirr to trouble
himself over whether or not his wife's name, Lucy, is "pretty."
"Pretty" simply doesn't signify for MacWhirr in that context.
Mrs. MacWhirr's name is a fact and no further effort on the
matter is required.

So, too, MacWhirr is hopelessly puzzled and even somewhat ill at ease in the presence of a metaphor. Jukes complains
of the heat, which is unbearable, even on deck: "It's the heat.
. . . The weather's awful. It would make a saint swear. Even up
here I feel exactly as if I had my head tied up in a woollen
blanket" (p. 25), only to be met with MacWhirr's totally blank:
"D'ye mean to say, Mr. Jukes, you ever had your head tied up
in a blanket? What was that for?" (p. 25).

MacWhirr's course of action for meeting the hurricane—"Keep her facing it—always facing it"—is intrepid and logical and ultimately successful, but it is also, admittedly, somewhat unimaginative. MacWhirr's stolidity here borders on stodginess. And yet, MacWhirr's action is wholly predictable, since he is unable to form any sort of mental concept of the extent of the danger which the storm poses. "Omens," says Conrad, "were as nothing to him, and he was unable to discover the message of a prophecy till the fulfillment had brought it home to his very door" (p. 6). (MacWhirr, one assumes, would also have trouble unraveling the burden of the metaphor which Conrad employs in the preceding quote.)

There is, finally, the incident of the Siamese flag, and Mac-Whirr is almost comic here in his complete inability to fathom the point Jukes seeks to make. The point, it might be noted, is not really all that subtle. Jukes means that the Siamese flag is "wrong" in flying over a British ship, while the literal MacWhirr construes that there is something wrong with the design of the flag and makes a point to reassure himself that the elephant is in the right place.

Thus, for all his admirable dedication to his ship and to his trust, for all the dispatch and the efficiency with which he handles his ship during the storm, MacWhirr is not entirely satisfactory as a model of fidelity. He is incomplete in his ability to wonder or even to doubt, and he is something less than human in his almost bloodless consistency. MacWhirr is, in fact, rather like the steamship he commands, mechanical and predictable. One is reminded of Conrad's description of the *Sofala* making her rounds, in *The End of the Tether:*

She could always be depended upon to make her courses. Her compasses were never out. . . . She made her landfalls to a degree of the bearing, and almost to a minute of her allowed time. (p. 506)

The comparison between man and ship gains validity if it is recalled that MacWhirr has been chosen by the Messrs. Sigg to command the *Nan-Shan* precisely because they have come to expect the same robot-like efficiency from him. Nor does Mac-Whirr fail them. It would be very difficult for the average seaman, however worthy, to emulate MacWhirr, simply because it would be impossible to identify with him.

At the other end of the scale stands Jim, preeminently a product, if not a victim, of his imagination. On several occasions, Marlow singles out Jim's "fatal gift" of an uncontrolled and uncontrollable imagination as the root of Jim's shortcomings and, most especially, as the key to his breach of the code aboard the *Patna*. Stein, too, recognizes the flaw—"He is romantic," which is, according to Stein, "very good" but also "very bad— very bad" (p. 132). Stein, with his superb grasp of essentials, realizes that Jim cannot always keep his eyes shut, as he does for a long period of time aboard the *Patna*. In order to "be," in the Steinian sense, Jim must see what actually is and not what his imagination tells him will be.

Marlow's summary of Jim's state of mind just before he leaps over the rail of the *Patna* is, of course, speculative, but it is relevant, and probably not very far from the truth:

"He was not afraid of death perhaps, but I'll tell you what, he was afraid of the emergency. His confounded imagination had evoked for him all the horrors of panic, the trampling rush, the pitiful screams, boats swamped—all the appalling incidents of a disaster at sea he had ever heard of." (p. 54)

And, a bit later, Marlow is able to see with Jim's eyes with such striking vividness that some questions might arise concerning the degree of control Marlow has over his own imagination:

"Nothing in the world moved before his eyes, and he could depict to himself without hindrance the sudden swing upwards of the dark skyline, the sudden tilt up of the vast plain of the sea, the swift still rise, the brutal fling, the grasp of the abyss, the struggle without hope, the starlight closing over his head for ever like the vault of a tomb—the revolt of his young life—the black end. He could! By Jove! who couldn't? And you must remember he was a finished artist in that peculiar way, he was a gifted poor devil with the faculty of swift and forestalling vision." (p. 59)

Quite clearly, Jim is also not acceptable as a model for the average seaman. And Jim is eliminated as exemplar not only because he is a failure but also because of his "fatal gift." But, whereas MacWhirr must be rejected as the ideal because his stolidity and his impassivity are simply beyond the scope of the average human being, Jim must be set aside for exactly opposite reasons. It would be very easy for the average seaman, however worthy he might otherwise be, to identify with Jim and, like Jim, to be victimized by "the faculty of swift and forestalling vision."

MacWhirr and Jim stand at opposite ends of the spectrum of the human condition: MacWhirr is unimaginative, to a degree dehumanized, but a success; Jim is overimaginative, very human indeed and, therefore, vulnerable and a failure.

Is there somewhere in Conrad a balance point, a Conradian seaman who is able to meet the exacting demands of the code without becoming a lifeless, nerveless, and humorless automaton? The obvious candidate is Charlie Marlow.

For all the recurrent breast-beating on Marlow's part that goes on in *Lord Jim* over his inability to "see" Jim clearly, it is evident that Marlow fully understands how Jim could be betrayed by his own imagination and that he even identifies with Jim on this score. For instance, Marlow is very well aware of what Jim is talking about as he relives the *Patna* episode in the privacy of Marlow's room in the Malabar House. It is Marlow, after all, who gives a name to Jim's malaise—"he was a gifted poor devil with the faculty of swift and forestalling vision"—and he is able to name it because he recognizes the common bond of vulnerability between himself and Jim. Marlow has insisted many times that Jim is "one of us," and here the phrase takes on another of the many meanings with which it is charged in the novel. Jim is "one of us" in that his case is not really all that rare. There is, for example, a bond between Jim and Brierly, whose imagination also betrays him in painting a mental picture with which Brierly cannot live. There is Jim's kinship with the French lieutenant, who is quite aware of the powers of the imagination but who has learned to sublimate the fear conjured up by the imagination under a MacWhirr-like impassivity. (Unlike MacWhirr, who is evidently aware of nothing, the lieutenant, of course, realizes that the fear is not really dissipated, merely dormant.) In fact, all the members of the fellowship of the craft of any sensitivity either share or have shared Jim's dilemma. Significantly, Jim has no last name, which further identifies him as Everyman. The point is that all worthy seamen have been assailed by the terrors of the imagination and by fear; Jim is different only in that he has fallen victim. The others have coped.

Marlow, too, has shared in this appointed burden of the craft—learning to live with the shadow of fear. It is revealing that whenever Jim arrives at the point of framing the question "What would you have done?" he seems to touch a Marlovian nerve. Marlow puts him off either by resorting to sarcasm or by abruptly leading the conversation in another direction. And Marlow's graphic evocation of Jim, in the course of telling Jim's story, is, perhaps, sufficient testimony to the powers of Marlow's imagination.

Marlow readily admits the difficulties attendant on overcoming fear—the burden of the craft—and on keeping faith— the condition of the craft. "I see well enough now," Marlow confesses in reference to Jim's case, "that I hoped for the impossible —for the laying of what is the most obstinate ghost of man's creation . . . the doubt of the sovereign power enthroned in a fixed standard of conduct" (p. 31).

But, much as Marlow may sympathize with Jim, even empathize with him, he does not excuse him. Much as Marlow is aware of the difficulties incumbent on the absolute adherence to "a fixed standard of conduct," this is precisely what Marlow demands of Jim. And he is justified in making this demand, for at least two reasons. In the first place, Jim has all the moral and physical equipment necessary to make and to keep this commitment. He is, again, "one of us," in yet another sense, and fidelity is expected of him, by Marlow and, indeed, by the craft itself. Second, Marlow asks no more of Jim than what he has himself done. Marlow has been to the heart of darkness; he has faced "the fascination of the abomination"; he has been tempted to respond to the drums sounding on the shore; he has lived in a world of imagined terrors, but he has coped and kept faith.

How does one cope? In Marlow's case and, as we will see, in other cases, too, the answer is work, devotion to duty, getting on with the job to the exclusion of all other diversions and distractions. As the steamboat makes its way upriver in *Heart of Dark-*

ness, for example, it is the redeeming power of work which spells salvation for the native fireman and for Marlow, for savage and civilized alike: "The snags were thick, the water was treacherous and shallow, the boiler seemed indeed to have a sulky devil in it, and thus neither that fireman nor I had any time to peer into our creepy thoughts" (p. 38). The chief virtue of work, it will be recalled from Marlow's pronouncement on the subject, is "the chance to find yourself. Your own reality—for yourself" (p. 29). Work, in other words, stills the inner voices that would speak to Marlow and turns his attention from the picture which the mind creates to the reality which exists. (In fairness to Jim, it must be conceded that he doesn't have much to occupy him aboard the _Patna_. It is a soft berth; his duties are not demanding; he has plenty of time to indulge in imaginings. Ultimately, Jim has so much time that, in the moment of crisis, he is free to "peer into his creepy thoughts" and mistake them for reality.)

The consanguinity of fidelity and work, to be seen in Marlow's case, leads to the observation that in Conrad's sea tales there is a rather extensive area in which the two concepts occupy common ground. When Singleton stays at the wheel of the _Narcissus_ for thirty hours, for instance, is he being faithful to a trust or is he the diligent worker doing his job diligently? When Captain Beard, in "Youth," insists on trimming the yards right after the explosion that nearly wrecks the ship, does he react from his sense of commitment to take the _Judea_ to Bangkok, or is he motivated by a desire to restore the ship's normal routine?

There are two statements from the sea stories which deserve quoting, since they lead to a valid distinction that may be made between fidelity, or trust, and work.

The first we have already seen. Baker, annoyed by the waywardness of the _Narcissus_'s crew, berates them thus: "Are you a lot of women passengers to be cared for? We are here to take care of the ship" (p. 364). In a like vein, there is this passage from _Typhoon_, in which Conrad speaks of the _Nan-Shan_'s engines:

This was their work—this patient coaxing of a distracted ship over the fury of the waves and into the very eye of the wind. At times Mr. Rout's chin would sink on his breast, and he watched them with knitted eyebrows as if lost in thought. (p. 73)

The latter part of the quotation has been included so that we do not lose sight of a salient point. It is by the license, by the care and concern of men, that the *Narcissus* beats the storm and the *Nan-Shan*'s engines *do* work and *do* drive the ship.

Work, then, is a condition or a concomitant of fidelity. It is by their capacity for and willingness to work that men keep faith. And, it is in direct ratio to their industriousness that men are faithful.

This cause and effect relationship between work and fidelity is admirably illustrated in "Youth," in a passage quoted earlier in this chapter. Beard has just run out on deck after the explosion and, stunned though he is, the discipline of years makes him instantly aware of the unmanned wheel. His first thought is the immediate job at hand, getting the *Judea* under control again and back on course, and this leads, in a natural causal relationship, to the larger consideration of keeping faith with the ship and bringing her safely to her destined port:

And, mark, he noticed directly the wheel deserted and his bark off her course—and his only thought was to get that miserable, stripped, undecked, smoldering shell of a ship back again with her head pointing at her port of destination. Bangkok! That's what he was after.
                                                                    (p. 136)

There are times, in Conrad, when work serves an even higher end, when it is not only the means to fidelity and the successful completion of the seaman's basic mission, but also the means to the worker's salvation, either physical or spiritual. By way of illustration, consider the situation aboard the *Narcissus* after the storm has largely passed and the ship has righted herself and is responding again to the helm. The crew are sprawled about her deck half-dead with fatigue and contemplating some very welcome rest for the very weary. But the *Narcissus* is still in some danger, and the men, as Allistoun with the wisdom of long experience recognizes, are in even greater danger. They are in danger of the lassitude and the collapse of the will which sets in after an emotional peak. Faced with the prospect of losing both men and ship, Allistoun proposes to cure the crew's physical and spiritual weariness by the seemingly insane, but actually quite sound device of more work:

> "Get sail on the ship. . . . Get sail on her as soon as you can.
> This is a fair wind. At once, sir—don't give the men time to feel
> themselves. They will get done up and stiff, and we will never. . . .
> We must get her along now. . . . Make sail." (p. 374)

In this instance, it is difficult to say whether the men or the ship
are the ultimate beneficiary.

Work is a painful antidote for fatigue, but it can be a necessary one when the alternative is even less attractive. As an illustration, we may turn again to the deck of the *Narcissus,* this time
during the height of the storm. Five men have gone into the deck-
house, which is half under water, in order to rescue Jimmy Wait.
They are thwarted by a series of misadventures and nearly dis-
traught with the fear of being trapped along with Jimmy should
the ship go over. Most maddening of all, however, is the sound of
Wait's screams. The thought of giving up crosses their minds:

> The agony of his fear wrung our hearts so terribly that we longed to
> abandon him, to get out of that place deep as a well and swaying
> like a tree, to get out of his hearing, back on the poop where we
> could wait passively for death in incomparable repose. (p. 352)

The alternative to getting on with the work, it appears, is a
placid resignation that is almost certainly accompanied by dis-
solution.

The redeeming virtue of work may be observed again in a
brief episode from *Typhoon* in which the alternative to work is
seen in terms which borrow heavily from the ancient saw about
idle hands being the devil's playthings. Solomon Rout, the chief
engineer of the *Nan-Shan,* is so occupied during the hurricane
that he, like Marlow in *Heart of Darkness,* has no time to peer
into his "creepy thoughts." As Jukes makes his way through the
engine room to reach the 'tween-deck, Rout does, however, find
a moment for a bit of banter in keeping with the traditional good-
humored rivalry between deck and engine room. His comments
contain a considerable truth wrapped in a jest:

"Go away now, for God's sake. You deck people'll drive me silly. . . . You fellows are going wrong for want of something to do." (p. 75)

One immediately thinks of Jim, who may very well have gone wrong for want of something to do.

To his good fortune, Jukes, the chief mate of the *Nan-Shan*, has more than enough to do when the typhoon hits. Unlike Mac-Whirr, Jukes has a perfectly healthy imagination and, at the outset, it bids fair to play him false:

Though young, he had seen some bad weather, and had never doubted his ability to imagine the worst; but this was so much beyond his powers of fancy that it appeared incompatible with the existence of any ship whatever. (p. 41)

When Jukes becomes fully aware of the magnitude of the threat which faces the *Nan-Shan*, he is momentarily paralyzed and can do no more than to repeat mentally, "My God! My God! My God! My God!" (p. 42), which immediately prompts comparison with MacWhirr's low-key moment of truth, "I wouldn't like to lose her." Jukes is thus in imminent danger of falling victim to his fears, fears which are half real and half imagined: "A dull conviction seized upon Jukes that there was nothing to be done" (p. 45); "Something within him seemed to turn over, bringing uppermost the feeling that the *Nan-Shan* was lost" (p. 45). At length, a crisis is reached: "Directly, his heart, corrupted by the storm that breeds a craving for peace, rebelled against the tyranny of training and command" (p. 53). Ironically, what Jukes is rebelling against is the wherewithal of his salvation. MacWhirr has ordered him to straighten out the melee going on among the coolies on the 'tween-deck. And there is a double irony in the fact that the coolies, whom Jukes holds in considerable contempt, should provide him with the means to save himself. Jukes's salvation is wrought, of course, through the task which MacWhirr has assigned him. Reaching the 'tween-deck on a ship very nearly out of control keeps Jukes sufficiently occupied so that his fears and his imagination are subsumed in the physical and mental effort required to carry out his orders. And even when Jukes falters momentarily on reaching the bunker adjacent to the 'tween-deck, the demands of the work to be done are there as a saving corrective: "He had half a mind to scramble out again; but the remembrance of Captain MacWhirr's voice made this impossible" (p. 62).

But for the ultimate example of the therapeutic value of work, we must turn again to the ubiquitous Charlie Marlow. As we have seen, it is Marlow who gives voice to the most cogent statement of the saving grace of work. There are, however, other reasons for singling out Marlow. There is, for instance, the central role which work plays in the drama of *Heart of Darkness*. Striking as the redemptions of the crew of the *Narcissus* and of Jukes are, they are secondary issues in their respective stories. In *The Nigger of the "Narcissus,"* Conrad's chief concern is the two deaths which occur, the death of Jimmy Wait and the death of the ship. In *Typhoon*, Conrad's attention is focused on his admirable but flawed hero, MacWhirr. In *Heart of Darkness*, however, Marlow's salvation through work is the story's raison d'être.

We might also establish the central nature of work as salvation in Marlow's case by considering the ultimate dispositions made of the three major figures in *Heart of Darkness* and *Lord Jim*—Kurtz, Jim, and Marlow. All three are tested severely. Kurtz fails and is destroyed utterly; Jim is deceived and made more vulnerable, and this vulnerability becomes fatal in his encounter with Gentleman Brown on Patusan; Marlow, however, is enlarged and enlightened by his test, and the essential difference in the three instances is that Marlow alone recognizes and capitalizes on his need for "rivets."

It is evident, then, that the craft demands a good deal of its followers in its insistence on uncompromising fidelity and on rigorous and diligent devotion to duty, a diligence which usually takes the unheroic and unappetizing guise of work. The seaman who would be faithful and would be diligent is not, however, without some resources from which he may seek comfort and support. There is, for instance, the long tradition of the craft, and chiefly the example of the faithful and diligent members of the fellowship who have gone before him and with whom he has natural and immutable ties. This is "the strong bond of the sea" of which Marlow speaks in "Youth" (p. 115), and it serves the seaman in two ways: it is both a glorious past in which he may take pride and a living present in which he may find sustenance.

Conrad evokes the past splendidly in *The Mirror of the Sea* in recalling his first encounter with the sea, the Mediterranean of southern France. The ancient and the honorable nature of the craft is set forth in terms which cannot fail to strike a resonant chord in the heart and mind of any worthy seaman:

The cradle of oversea traffic and of the art of naval combats, the Mediterranean, apart from all the associations of adventure and glory, the common heritage of all mankind, makes a tender appeal to a seaman. It has sheltered the infancy of his craft. He looks upon it as a man may look at a vast nursery in an old, old mansion where innumerable generations of his own people have learned to walk. I say his own people because, in a sense, all sailors belong to one family: all are descended from that adventurous and shaggy ancestor who, bestriding a shapeless log and paddling with a crooked branch, accomplished the first coasting trip in a sheltered bay ringing with the admiring howls of his tribe. (pp. 148–49)

The same pride, somewhat updated, is seen again in *The Nigger of the "Narcissus"* as Conrad, prompted by the figure of Singleton as shining example, turns his attention to the "happy breed of men" for whom he would naturally feel a special affection, the generation of seamen who went to sea under sail:

. . . they had been men who knew toil, privation, violence, debauchery—but knew not fear, and had no desire of spite in their hearts. . . . Their generation lived inarticulate and indispensable, without knowing the sweetness of affections or the refuge of a home—and died free from the dark menace of a narrow grave. They were the everlasting children of the mysterious sea. . . . They are gone now—and it does not matter. The sea and the earth are unfaithful to their children: a truth, a faith, a generation of men goes—and is forgotten, and it does not matter! Except, perhaps, to the few of those who believed the truth, confessed the faith—or loved the men.
(pp. 313–14)

But the seaman's feeling for tradition, which is so important a part of the craft, is not static; it is not confined to contemplating a fixed and immutable past to which perfunctory homage is paid. Rather, it is an active and vital presence to which the seaman may turn for solace and for inspiration.

As the youthful Marlow, in "Youth," approaches the East, for example, he is very much aware of the seagoing adventurers who have preceded him and he exults in the knowledge that he has found a place in their ranks:

> There was all the East before me, and all life, and the thought that I had been tried in that ship and had come out pretty well. And I thought of men of old who, centuries ago, went that road in ships that sailed no better, to the land of palms, and spices, and yellow sands, and of brown nations ruled by kings more cruel than Nero the Roman, and more splendid than Solomon the Jew. (pp. 129–30)

Tradition as a vital force may be seen again in *A Personal Record*. In this instance, the tie between present and past is more direct, since it is not simply a matter of being inspired by or taking heart from the example of the past. Rather, the consignment of the inherited wisdom of the past from one generation to the next is involved. Conrad has been describing his examination for his master's ticket and he turns his attention, for a moment, to the examiner. What chiefly emerges in the passages which follow is the continuity of the craft, the master mariners who are about to pass from the scene, creating, by a figurative laying-on of hands, the master mariners who will take their places in the never-depleted ranks:

> Clearly the transport service had been the making of this examiner, who so unexpectedly had given me an insight into his existence, awakening in me the sense of the continuity of that sea-life into which I had stepped from outside; giving a touch of human intimacy to the machinery of official relations. I felt adopted. His experience was for me, too, as though he had been an ancestor. (p. 118)

> The era of examinations was over. I would never again see that friendly man who was a professional ancestor, a sort of grandfather in the craft. (p. 119)

Perhaps the most memorable expression of the continuity of the craft comes in *The Shadow-Line*. The young captain, who has literally had command thrust upon him, sits for the first time in the master's chair, which faces an ancient mirrored sideboard.

The wardroom is deserted, but the captain is immediately aware
that he is not really alone. He is suddenly conscious of all the
men who have sat in that chair before him, men to whom he may
turn for understanding, but also, to whom he will be answerable:

> A succession of men had sat in that chair. I became aware of
> that thought suddenly, vividly, as though each had left a little of him-
> self between the four walls of these ornate bulkheads; as if a sort of
> composite soul, the soul of command, had whispered suddenly to
> mine of long days at sea and of anxious moments.
> ... Deep within the tarnished ormolu frame, in the hot half-light
> sifted through the awning, I saw my own face propped between my
> hands. And I stared back at myself with the perfect detachment of
> distance, rather with curiosity than with any other feeling, except
> of some sympathy for this latest representative of what for all in-
> tents and purposes was a dynasty; continuous not in blood, indeed
> but in its experience, in its training, in its conception of duty, and
> in the blessed simplicity of its traditional point of view on life.
>
> (pp. 52–53)

For the best statement of the role which a feeling for tradition plays and has played in defining and shaping the fellowship of
the craft, we must turn again to Charlie Marlow. In *Lord Jim*
Marlow leaves his story briefly in order to offer his credentials as
a kind of recruiting agent-at-large for prospective members of
the fellowship. The issue is important at this point in the novel
since it establishes how far divergent appearance and reality are
in Jim's case. Jim fools even a trained observer. But the point
becomes almost secondary in the midst of Conrad's finest tribute
to his youthful calling. In Conrad-Marlow's celebration of the
traditions and the heritage of the craft, two points are stressed:
the sense of continuity, of a vital inheritance being passed down
in an unbroken line, is seen again; second, it becomes evident from
the enthusiasm with which Marlow speaks that his occasional role
as mentor and guide to future members of the craft has been the
most rewarding experience of his seagoing career. In pronouncing
his eulogy, Marlow predicates a hypothetical encounter with
"some sunburnt young chief mate" (p. 27) whom Marlow has
introduced to the sea, perhaps a decade earlier. There is, to begin
with in Marlow's remarks, a touch of nonchalance, largely
feigned, when he reduces the nurturing process of the craft to a

"fool game," but the sincerity and the satisfaction soon show through:

> . . . the man who had taken a hand in this fool game, in which the sea wins every toss, will be pleased to have his back slapped by a heavy young hand, and to hear a cheery sea-puppy voice: "Do you remember me, sir? The little So-and-so."
> I tell you this is good; it tells you that once in your life at least you have gone the right way to work. I have been thus slapped, and I have winced, for the slap was heavy, and I have glowed all day long and gone to bed feeling less lonely in the world by virtue of that hearty thump. (p. 28)

To recapitulate briefly, the great secret of the craft of which Conrad, speaking through Marlow, makes a good deal, turns out to be no secret at all. It is, rather, common knowledge which every seaman shares—that the sole mission of the craft is to keep ships afloat and bring them safely to port. Fulfilling this mission, however, is something else again and not so simple a matter. It involves an almost impossibly rigorous adherence to a fixed standard of conduct, an equally demanding dedication to duty, and a proper understanding of and respect for the heritage of the craft. Through their unstinting efforts, and, with a fillip of luck, most of Conrad's seamen succeed. There are, however, notable failures, as we have seen; and, as we shall see, these become the objects of Conrad's special consideration.

CHAPTER FIVE

THE SEAMEN

Who would be a sailor if he could be a farmer?
                    —*The Nigger of the "Narcissus"*

For surely it is a great thing to have commanded a handful
of men worthy of one's undying regard.
                    —"Author's Note" to *The Shadow-Line*

The Children of the Sea.   —Title of first American edition
                    of *The Nigger of the "Narcissus"*

The first point to be remarked of Conrad's seamen is that
very few of them were born to the sea and are thus professional
sailors in the strictest sense of the phrase. In fact, of the many
mariners who caught Conrad's fancy, retained a hold in his
memory, and found their way into the pages of his sea stories,
only two—Tom Lingard and Captain Allistoun of the *Narcissus*
—really qualify, since they come from seagoing families and,
accordingly, have natural ties with the sea. The rest of Conrad's
seamen fall into two categories: the gentlemen-professionals, men
generally of good birth who have been educated to the sea
through formal training, and the seamen of chance or expe-
dience, largely of middle-class origins, who have educated themselves to the sea through long and demanding experience.

Allistoun's credentials as a seaman by the right of birth are
impressive. He was born, we are told, "on the shores of the
Pentland Firth" (*The Nigger of the "Narcissus,"* p. 318), the
northernmost strait in Scotland. Here the North Sea and the
Atlantic, coming into confluence, join to create perhaps the

oughest and most treacherous waters for small boats to be ound anywhere in the world. With the Firth as his "nursery of he craft," Allistoun was well equipped for anything the sea night have to offer him, and his later career is evidence of the horoughness of his apprenticeship. But the Firth was only the beginning of Allistoun's training for the sea, his primary grades, so to speak. Advanced training came in the Peterhead whalers, where, Conrad reports, Allistoun attained the rank of harpooner, no modest feat for a relatively young man. The rigorous and exacting nature of Allistoun's schooling for the sea was, of course, altogether fitting for one of the craft's elite, one who had, in effect, inherited the sea; but Allistoun clearly looks back on those early days with something less than enthusiasm. When he spoke of his service in the whaling fleet, we are informed, "his restless gray eyes became still and cold, like the loom of ice" (p. 318). *Odi et amo,* Conrad has said, is the characteristic feeling of the seaman toward the world of his calling, and Allistoun shares with his colleagues of the craft this admixture of attraction and repugnance. And if Allistoun views the past with mixed emotions, so too there is a duality in his vision of the future. He has now arrived at the zenith of the professional seaman's expectations; he commands a crack ship and has commanded her since the day of her christening; he loves and trusts his ship, as a worthy seaman should, and, in his pride in his command, he drives his ship to the limits, hoping some day for a record passage. Yet, exemplary as Allistoun's career is and gratified as he may be at being master of the *Narcissus,* his idea of ultimate bliss is a quiet retirement in a little house with a plot of ground "far in the country—out of sight of the sea" (p. 319).

Lingard, too, has been born to the deck and the bridge. Like Allistoun, he comes from a long line of seafarers, or, as Conrad puts it, Lingard is the "child of generations of fishermen from the coast of Devon" (*The Rescue,* pp. 10–11). And, like Allistoun, Lingard has undergone the same ritual of trial and ordeal—"Brixham trawler-boy, afterward a youth in colliers, deep-water man" (p. 78)—to prepare him for the family inheritance which will fall to him, a life at sea. Here, however, the resemblance between the West-country boy and the proper, taciturn Scot who commands the *Narcissus* ends. For, though by all reckoning Lingard is destined for a career as a Devon fisherman or for a lifetime of service in the merchant fleet, there is a touch of the maverick in him which prompts him to abandon the simple life of his forefathers or the traditional career in the home service which is his natural lot. This unconventional son of very conventional Devon fishermen finds the East and becomes Tom Lingard, trader, adventurer, and seaman extraordinary, and his life is such as Allistoun, and all proper seamen, can only dream of. As the Rajah Laut, "the King of the Sea," founder of the settlement on the River Pantai and friend to the Wajo people, Lingard is himself one of the mysteries of the East.

But, for all the exoticism which surrounds him, Lingard is, nonetheless, a professional seaman of the highest competence. He handles the brig *Lightning* with a skill and daring that is the envy of even those who deplore his flair for showmanship. Further, between Lingard and his ship there is a relationship which is almost mystical and certainly in keeping with the best traditions of the craft. Lingard is guilty of only the slightest hyperbole in his frequent unspoken assertion that he "cared for nothing *living* but the brig" (p. 10). And there is no exaggeration at all in his avowal, "If I lost her I would have no standing room on the earth for my feet" (p. 229). But the best testimony to Lingard's seamanship and his professionalism is the fact that he is able to take the *Lightning* where no other white man is able to go or dares to go. It is true, of course, that Lingard is the only white man who is persona grata at Sambir or on the Shore of Refuge, but it is also true that he is the only white man who knows the reefs and the currents and the reaches and, finally, who knows his ship well enough to risk the passages.

But seamen such as Allistoun and Lingard, who are virtually born at sea and who embrace the craft as a birthright are the exceptions in Conrad. More common are men of good family, perhaps second or third sons, who have no natural ties with the sea and are educated to the craft. These are the gentlemen professionals who go to sea enjoying a status comparable to the modern midshipman. They are trained seamen, rather

than natural seamen, but they are, nevertheless, often fine
seamen.

One of these seamen by training rather than by instinct is
Marlow's host and drinking companion, the Director of Companies, whom Marlow identifies as a *Conway* boy, a graduate of
the training ship which functioned for Conrad as a kind of
grammar school, turning out worthy members of the craft. Invariably, in Conrad, to be a *Conway* boy is a hallmark of excel-
lence and competence. Jim is the one noteworthy failure, as-
suming, of course (and it is a reasonable assumption), that the
training ship on which Jim prepares for the sea is this selfsame
Conway.

In "The Secret Sharer," it will be recalled, two other gentlemen professionals, the young captain and Leggatt, discover that
they are both graduates of the *Conway,* although separated by
several years so that their terms aboard the training ship did not
coincide. Immediately on the discovery of their common bond,
the rapport between the two deepens and, even more important
for the story, the leavening of the old school tie increases the
captain's growing sense of commitment to Leggatt. The *Conway,*
in effect, serves as a universal letter of credit and provides an
entree in much the same manner as does the service academy
ring today. It is virtually impossible for the captain to believe
that a *Conway* boy could be guilty of a brutal murder, and he
accepts Leggatt's version of the events aboard the *Sephora* in
much the same way that one would accept the "word" of an
officer and gentleman. Yet, while both Leggatt and the captain
have been trained to the sea in the same school, the ultimate
force of being a *Conway* boy is not so much the common experience; rather, the designation immediately establishes the
captain and Leggatt as sharers of another inheritance. They are
both, in Marlow's words, "one of us."

Jim, another gentleman professional, would also enjoy this
immediate acceptance were it not for the *Patna* disgrace. Indeed,
as we have noted earlier, Marlow indicates that he would not
hesitate to accept Jim on the face of his appearance and on the
basis of his credentials, not the least of which is his *Conway*
background. And, there are other reasons for accepting Jim. He

comes from a solid, substantial family (Jim is the son of a parson), as do the captain and Leggatt; and one may assume that in
all three cases, choice or necessity has dictated their finding their
way to the sea via the *Conway*. In Jim's case, one presumes that
his career at sea was governed by both motivations, choice and
necessity. Jim, it will be remembered, had engaged in "a course
of light holiday literature" which attracted him to the sea and
later contributed to his undoing. At the same time, the modest
resources of a country vicarage no doubt left the parson's son
with a limited number of options in determining his career.

Jim, in many ways, epitomizes the trained gentleman-sailor.
He is of the proper kind of family, with the proper professional
background aboard the *Conway;* he has the proper physical
equipment and the proper look about him. He is, in fact, so preeminently "one of us" in appearance that when he falls from
grace Marlow is compelled to come to his aid, and only partly
for Jim's sake. Marlow adopts Jim, in effect, for the sake of all
the *Conway* boys who have been accepted into the craft and
ultimately, perhaps, for the sake of the craft itself.

Of the origins and background of Charlie Marlow nothing
is known, and this is striking in view of the care Conrad otherwise takes in delineating and individualizing his seaman-persona.
Moreover, such singular reticence is rather out of character on
Marlow's part, since he is so garrulous, if not patently long-
winded, on so many other subjects. In the absence of specifics,
however, it is pleasant and it does no harm to think of Marlow
as a *Conway* boy and a product of some such background as
that which produced Jim and Leggatt, the Director of Companies, and the captain of "The Secret Sharer."

The majority of Conrad's seamen, however, are neither
born to the sea nor formally trained to the sea. Rather, they
gravitate toward the sea and toward ships, sometimes through
chance but more often through necessity. Once at sea, they
undergo a period of apprenticeship which has much in common
with the medieval crafts and guilds system and is a nineteenth-
century forerunner of on-the-job training. These are Marlow's
"Little So-and-so's"; they go aboard ship at a very early age,
from no great conviction, and are committed to their seagoing

calling almost before they are capable of exercising any choice. Indeed, in many instances they become fellows of the craft involuntarily. Marlow, in looking back on his years as unofficial training master, depicts vividly the typical beginning of such a career before the mast:

And I would remember a bewildered little shaver, no higher than the back of this chair, with a mother and perhaps a big sister on the quay, very quiet but too upset to wave their handkerchiefs at the ship that glides out gently between the pier-heads; or perhaps some decent, middle-aged father who had come early with his boy to see him off, and stays all the morning because he is interested in the windlass apparently. . . . All very proper. He has offered his bit of sacrifice to the sea, and now he may go home pretending he thinks nothing of it; and the little willing victim will be very seasick before next morning. (*Lord Jim,* p. 28)

The seamen who have gone to sea in this rather impromptu and totally unglamorous fashion are to be found again and again in Conrad's sea tales. The redoubtable Captain MacWhirr, for instance, by all rights should have measured out his days as a greengrocer in Belfast, following in the footsteps of his tradesman father. Yet, at the age of fifteen, inexplicably and wonderfully, MacWhirr had gone off to sea, to the continuing chagrin of his family. And Conrad is at as much of a loss to explain MacWhirr's vagary as is the elder MacWhirr. "It was enough, when you thought it over," says Conrad, "to give you the idea of an immense, potent, and invisible hand thrust into the ant-heap of the earth, laying hold of shoulders, knocking heads together, and setting the unconscious faces of the multitude towards inconceivable goals and in undreamt-of directions" (*Typhoon,* pp. 4–5).

Similarly, Captain Beard of the *Judea* has come up through the ranks—"years in coasters, then in the Mediterranean, and last in the West Indian trade" ("Youth," p. 117)—and has reached the pinnacle of command only at the advanced age of sixty. Captain Whalley, presumably, has undergone the same apprenticeship at sea, but he has been more resourceful or luckier than Beard, since he has had his own command for a number of years prior to his retirement. Montagu Brierly, even more resourceful or more lucky, has arrived at the command of the *Ossa* at the age of thirty-two, but there is nothing to suggest that Brierly's apprentice years were any different, merely truncated. And the list of Conrad's seamen who came to the sea young and learned their craft in the school of practical experience could be multiplied at length: Mr. Baker of the *Narcissus,* Jukes of the *Nan-Shan,* Solomon Rout of the *Nan-Shan,* Singleton, Carter in *The Rescue,* Mr. Burns in *The Shadow-Line,* Mr. Jones, chief mate of the *Ossa,* Mr. Mahon of the *Judea,* Archbold of the *Sephora.*

A number of Conrad's seamen share a particular milieu as a background, one which seems, at first glance, the least likely source for recruitment into the craft. Both Jim and Leggatt are parson's sons, and Conrad says of parsonages: "Many commanders of fine merchant-ships come from these abodes of piety and peace" (*Lord Jim,* p. 4). The placid, monotonous, and rather unsophisticated existence of the country parsonage would appear to be eons removed and worlds apart from the sometimes turbulent, often boisterous, and frequently rough-and-tumble life aboard a ship at sea. At the same time, a moment's reflection makes evident that the sons of parsons who go to sea bring with them a number of qualities which stand them in good stead to meet the demands of the craft. For one thing, they have come from families which place a premium on the twin virtues of discipline and hard work; they are accustomed to living something of a Spartan existence; finally, and most important, having grown up with a strong sense of the Christian ethic, they have less difficulty than most in adhering to "a fixed standard of conduct."

Which of the three routes to the sea is the best? Something can be said for each. The seaman who inherits his craft has fewer adjustments to make; the seaman who is trained to the sea enjoys certain social and professional advantages; the seaman who learns by doing is, perhaps, the most proficient, since he acquires his trade firsthand, from the fundamentals on up. Conrad ultimately passes no judgment on this score. In fact, it is clear from the evidence of the sea tales that good seamen may come from any quarter. Allistoun and Lingard are thorough professionals,

ut then, so are Leggatt and Marlow; and yet none of these, in
urn, is more worthy of the term "professional" than are the
nany self-made seamen, MacWhirr and Beard and Whalley and
ll the others.

On more than one occasion in the sea stories and in his two
utobiographical memoirs, Conrad comes out strongly for the
roposition that faithful service, like virtue, is its own reward.
Ierein Conrad is echoing Mr. Baker of the *Narcissus;* the sea-
nan is there to serve the ship, and serving well and diligently
s the sum and all of the craft. Marlow, in fact, faults Jim on
his very score. Jim, imbued as he is with the romantic notions he
nas carried over from his "course in light holiday literature,"
xpects too much from the sea (and, perhaps, gives too little).
im sees the sea as a kind of theater wherein he is destined "to
hine in the midst of dangers" (p. 5), whereas the sea, as Marlow
nd Conrad and all seamen know, is more often humble than
neroic. What redeems the drudgery and the sacrifice is not really
he infrequent moments of high drama but, rather, the simple
atisfaction of doing the job well, of keeping the ship safe. Mar-
ow remarks of Jim's early voyages (and there is a touch of ex-
speration in his tone):

. . he had to bear the criticism of men, the exactions of the sea,
nd the prosaic severity of the daily task that gives bread—but
vhose only reward is in the perfect love of the work. This reward
luded him. (p. 7)

The theme of selfless service is picked up again in a passage
from *The Mirror of the Sea* in which a number of the virtues of
:he craft—fidelity, tradition, professional competence—are
touched upon. The principal emphasis, however, falls on what
I have called elsewhere "the saving grace of work," and what
Conrad terms "the honor of labor":

Now, the moral side of an industry, productive or unproductive,
the redeeming and ideal aspect of this bread-winning, is the attain-
ment and preservation of the highest possible skill on the part of
the craftsmen. Such skill, the skill of technique, is more than honesty; it is something wider, embracing honesty and grace and rule
in an elevated and clear sentiment, not altogether utilitarian, which

may be called the honor of labor. It is made up of accumulate
tradition, kept alive by individual pride, rendered exact by profes
sional opinion, and, like the higher arts, it is spurred on and sus
tained by discriminating praise. (p. 24)

The very most by way of material reward that the seaman ca:
hope for or should hope for, or so Conrad notes in the closin;
sentence of the passage, is an occasional "well done," the tradi
tional accolade of the sea.

Yet, for all his celebration of the intangibles, of the satis
faction and gratification to be found in selfless service to th
craft, Conrad is often curiously preoccupied with the materia
and utilitarian rewards which the craft has to offer. Chief of thes
rewards, in Conrad's mind the ultimate boon which the seaman'
calling can bestow, is the command of a ship. Again and agai
in the sea tales, one finds Conrad dwelling on and even savorin;
the burdens and glories of command, its trappings, its mystique
its rationale. No less than three of Conrad's sea tales, "Youth,'
"The Secret Sharer," and *The Shadow-Line,* deal directly witl
problems of command. In each of these stories, a central char
acter has assumed command of a vessel for the first time. Indeed
it might be proposed that Conrad was more than a bit biased
as between the deck and the bridge. Only in *The Nigger of the
"Narcissus"* and in *Typhoon* do we get a glimpse of life in the
forecastle and meet some of the ordinary seamen who spin ou
their lives on and below decks. Otherwise, in Conrad's sea tale:
the attention is centered on the ship's officers and on the ward
room or the bridge, and most of the scenes are played in officers
country.

Much is made in *Typhoon* of the perquisites and the requi
sites of command. MacWhirr has the absolute confidence of the
Nan-Shan's owners, commands a fine ship, has earned the respec
of his officers and men, enjoys the rare privilege of being paic
for doing what he loves to do, and is in the even rarer positior
of being answerable to no one while his ship is at sea. And then
of course, there are the minor appurtenances which go with being
in command. The captain is served first at the wardroom table
and is deferred to, by custom if not by right, in all other instances
In the case of MacWhirr, his chartroom is maintained in spit-

nd-polish order by the steward and is kept to MacWhirr's precise
pecifications. There is, for instance, the box of matches placed
)n the chartroom shelf—"A box . . . just there, see? Not so
'ery full . . . where I can put my hand on it, steward" (p. 85)—
ind there is the water bottle and two tumblers, also positioned
iccording to MacWhirr's orders. Trivial matters, perhaps, but it
t obvious that Conrad is fascinated by these minute talismans of
:ommand.

It is equally evident, however, that Conrad is also aware of
he other side of the coin, of the unending demands and re-
:ponsibilities of command. In *Typhoon*, for instance, when it
)ecomes evident that the *Nan-Shan* is in for more than the com-
non run of heavy weather, Conrad describes Jukes as being
'uncritically glad to have his captain at hand. It relieved him
is though that man had, by simply coming on deck, taken most
)f the gale's weight upon his shoulders." "Such," says Conrad,
'is the prestige, the privilege, and the burden of command" (p.
39). A moment later, Conrad strikes a poignant note in reporting
that, in turn, "Captain MacWhirr could expect no relief of that
sort from anyone on earth." "Such," Conrad concludes, "is the
loneliness of command" (p. 40), and his conclusion bespeaks
his keen awareness of the inescapable nature of command responsibility.

Similarly, in *Typhoon*, when the boatswain discovers the
donnybrook going on among the coolies on the 'tween-deck, the
problem, as does any problem that might arise aboard the *Nan-
Shan*, becomes MacWhirr's to solve. The extent of the boatswain's obligation is to report the occurrence and, Conrad remarks somewhat dryly, "on board ship there is only one man
to whom it is worth while to unburden yourself" (p. 58). The
boatswain, having fought his way to the bridge, hangs on to
MacWhirr's coat desperately in a posture that is almost a direct
physical translation of his dependence on his captain, and makes
his report. Once he has placed the matter in the hands which
wield ultimate authority, the boatswain, Conrad writes, "subsided on the deck in a sitting posture. . . . He gave no more
thought to the coolies" (p. 59).

This same preoccupation with the problems of command is

encountered again in "The Secret Sharer." This, one of the bes
and best known of Conrad's short stories, is generally read as a
study of emerging self-awareness or self-understanding or ever
self-confidence on the part of the young captain, and the tex
adequately supports some such reading as this. For example, a
the outset of the story, when the captain is embarking on his firs
voyage as master of a ship, he is prone to wonder how far he
"should turn out faithful to that ideal conception of one's owr
personality every man sets up for himself secretly" (p. 651). Wha
has sometimes been overlooked in this reading is that the "idea
conception" the captain has set up is a vision of himself in a com
mand capacity, and his concern is that he measure up to thi
prefigured standard. At the end of the story, having fulfilled hi
commitment to Leggatt and tested his ship and himself, the cap
tain, presumably, has a better awareness and understanding of hi
own abilities and greater confidence in these abilities. Thus, the
captain's personal development is inextricably bound up with hi
growth as a professional seaman and, principally, as a seamar
capable of exercising command. What has really been at stake ir
the story is not so much the intangibles of the captain's "person
ality," as he calls it, as the concrete issue of his credentials fo
command. Again, we may turn to the text for our evidence. Jus
before he leaves the ship, Leggatt warns the young captain to ex
ercise care, and, seemingly for the first time, the captain recog
nizes how much he is risking and has been risking all along: "I
realized suddenly that all my future, the only future for which I
was fit, would perhaps go irretrievably to pieces in any mishap to
my first command" (p. 691). Paradoxically, it is by his willing
ness to risk his command that the captain enhances his capacity
for command.

The most thorough study of the conditions and concomitants
of command to be found in Conrad is *The Shadow-Line*. This is
Conrad's tale of the young first mate who leaves his ship in Singapore and leaves the sea for a time, as he supposes, only to have
command thrust upon him. The young mate is, quite literally,
turned into a ship's master in the space of a few hours. Initially,
and understandably, the new captain is overwhelmed by his abrupt
transition from executing orders to originating orders. He goes

through a period of self-probing and self-analysis more pronounced than that of the hero of "The Secret Sharer." In the midst of the unlucky voyage from Bangkok to Singapore, for instance, during which his crew are stricken with fever and his ship plagued by tricky winds, the captain's will nearly fails, and he confides his doubts and his fears to his diary:

It's like being bound hand and foot preparatory to having one's throat cut. And what appalls me most of all is that I shrink from going on deck to face it. It's due to the ship, it's due to the men who are there on deck. . . . And I am shrinking from it. From the mere vision. My first command. Now I understand that strange sense of insecurity in my past. I always suspected that I might be no good. And here is proof positive, I am shirking it, I am no good. (p. 107)

And, given his inexperience and the precipitousness of his rise to command, the captain makes mistakes, notably his failure to check the quinine supply personally, whereby he might have discovered his predecessor's venality in selling the quinine on the black market in Haiphong.

But, though the chief emphasis of *The Shadow-Line* falls on the captain's crossing the shadow line from youth to maturity and on his recognition of the burdens of command, the satisfactions of command, its gratifications and its joys, one might say, are not overlooked. Once he has decided to accept the vacant master's billet, the captain finds himself markedly elated. The trip to the Harbor Office where he will pick up his credentials is described glowingly:

It's a good step from the Officers' Home to the Harbor Office; but with the magic word "Command" in my head I found myself suddenly on the quay as if transported there in the twinkling of an eye, before a portal of dressed white stone above a flight of shallow white steps. (p. 28)

And the captain mentally contemplates his new command, which he has not yet seen, in terms which rise to the euphoric:

Captain Ellis (a fierce sort of fairy) had produced a command out of a drawer almost as unexpectedly as in a fairy tale. But a command is an abstract idea, and it seemed a sort of "lesser marvel" till it flashed upon me that it involved the concrete existence of a ship.

A ship! My ship! She was mine, more absolutely mine for possession and care than anything in the world; an object of responsibility and devotion. She was there waiting for me, spellbound, unable to move, to live, to get out into the world (till I came), like an enchanted princess. (p. 40)

Conrad's use of the metaphor of the fairy tale in these two passages is not out of place. For the worthy seaman, commanding one's own ship has something of a never-never quality, but still it is a dream which the seaman fervently hopes will come true.

Concurrent with Conrad's pronounced interest in the problems and privileges of command in the sea stories is an equal absorption with the plight of the perennial chief mates, those men who are fated never to stand on the bridge of their own ship. These seagoing runners-up in the race for command appear quite frequently in Conrad. They are to be encountered, for instance, in *The Mirror of the Sea* and in five of the sea tales, and they are subjects of more than passing concern on Conrad's part. Their appearance in such numbers may be accounted for in several ways: First, it reflects the economics of the craft in Conrad's day, when there were far more men holding master's tickets than there were ships to command. As a result, a number of highly qualified potential masters were destined to spend their careers at sea as first officers. Second, the liberal sprinkling of thwarted chief mates reflects Conrad's direct observation and experience. In twenty years at sea, Conrad no doubt encountered a good many of these disappointed men and they captured his imagination and his sympathies. Mr. B—, "the best of chief mates," is but one example who immediately comes to mind. Then, too, it must not be forgotten that Conrad himself served as a chief mate and underwent this same rigorous selection process, a point that we will return to in another context.

In some instances, it is relatively easy to ascertain why such-and-such a chief mate fails to capture the prize of command. The otherwise admirable Mr. B—, of *The Mirror of the Sea*, has a drinking problem, although, to be fair, he confines his drinking bouts to periods when his duties are not demanding, such as those times when the ship is in port. Shaw, Lingard's chief mate aboard the *Lightning,* may also be readily eliminated as a serious prospect for a command. In addition to his mean spirit, which, by itself, sufficiently compromises him, Shaw is completely lacking in principles. This, by a curious twist, is precisely the charge which Shaw raises against Lingard; and, given Shaw's warped thinking, there is a kind of logic in his ability to find his own shortcomings in others.

With Mr. Jones, in *Lord Jim,* and Mr. Burns, in *The Shadow-Line,* the faults which keep them from command are not as grievous, but they are no less disqualifying. Mr. Jones, of the crack ship *Ossa,* had fully expected to succeed Montagu Brierly when Brierly went over the side, taking his honors and his fears with him. He has, as he says, "been ten years in the Company, always expecting the next command—more fool I" (p. 37). The next command, at the time of Marlow's encounter with Jones, is the *Ossa,* and Jones is again disappointed. The Captain of the *Pelion*—"a little popinjay, in a grey check suit, with his hair parted in the middle" (p. 39), by Jones's account—is transferred to the vacant command and Jones remains a first mate. Jones's ill-tempered description of his new captain provides one of the clues to his failure to get on. He is, by universal reputation, an irascible and cantankerous man, and Marlow wonders how Brierly ever put up with him. The new captain of the *Ossa* calls Jones "an old ruffian" and assures him, "what's more, you are known for an old ruffian in the employ" (p. 39). This corroborating testimony (from Marlow and the captain) is good evidence that Jones's reputation as a terrible-tempered Mr. Bang of the sea is honestly come by. But Jones has another and more serious flaw. He is extremely naive and, evidently, not terribly bright. For instance, he is never able to grapple successfully with the subtleties of Marlow's solution to the Brierly mystery—that Brierly's trouble was the fear of failure or, to turn the coin, the fear of continuing success. Jones remains thoroughly mystified after his meeting with Marlow, and the best his limited imaginative resources can come up with is the almost ludicrous suggestion, "You would think, sir, he had jumped overboard only to give an unlucky man a last show to get on" (p. 39).

Mr. Burns, chief mate of the unnamed ship in *The Shadow-Line,* also hopes to get on. In fact, he takes active measures to further his cause by taking the ship to Bangkok, after the previous captain's death, instead of to Singapore, its port of destination. It requires only a little effort on the part of the new master to fathom Burns's motives: "He took the ship to a port where he expected to be confirmed in his temporary command from lack of a qualified master to put over his head. Whereas Singapore, he surmised justly, would be full of qualified men" (p. 63). As it turns out, there is not an oversupply of qualified men in Singapore, but there is one, the central character of *The Shadow-Line,* and Burns's scheme is thwarted when the new captain is dispatched to Bangkok to take command of the ship. Burns is, of course, duly resentful and resorts to the conventional gambit of announcing that only the fact he has a wife and children at home keeps him at his post. But Burns's shortcomings are more fundamental than his fit of pique at being passed over. Burns has buried the late captain at the entrance to the Gulf of Siam, at 8° 20′ latitude to be precise, the entry having been properly made in the log. When the ship is becalmed, ridden with fever and unable, it appears, to get well into the Gulf and on its way to Singapore, Burns becomes obsessed with the notion that the ship is cursed. It becomes an article of faith with him that the dead captain has bewitched the ship and will not let it pass beyond the latitude of his burial place. The intensity of Burns's idée fixe and his utter abandon in the face of it, raise serious questions about his judgment and his stability. It is true that Burns is himself stricken with fever throughout most of the voyage and thus, perhaps, not responsible for his actions. The clear impression given, however, is that even if he were perfectly fit, his preoccupation with ghosts and goblins would seriously compromise his efficiency and would, of course, be fatal were he in command.

That Jones and Burns are perennial chief mates is thus relatively easy to fathom. However, when we turn to Mahon, the chief mate of the *Judea,* and Baker, the second-in-command of the *Narcissus,* and endeavor to explain their failure to get on, we run into a number of anomalies and difficulties. By all accounts—by long service, by professional competence, by being, in general, among the worthiest of the seamen in the fellowship of the craft, both men should have been pacing the bridges of their own ships long since. Mahon, for instance, has had an exemplary career and is already expert in his craft when the young Marlow encounters him. (I do not overlook the fact that part of Conrad's purpose here is dramatic contrast. The twenty-year-old second mate, Marlow, sails on an old ship, the *Judea,* with an old captain [Beard is sixty and this is his first command] and an old chief mate, and the title of the story is "Youth.") Even the youthful and callow Marlow, however, pays tribute to Mahon's abilities. "He was," Marlow reports, "well connected; yet there was something wrong with his luck, and he had never got on" ("Youth," p. 117). In other words, Marlow can find no compelling reason for Mahon's failure to join the elite of the sea.

Similarly, it is difficult to account for Baker's lack of success. Conrad calls him "a model chief mate," but the point is that he remains a chief mate. Baker is generally a bit more contemplative and analytical than many of Conrad's chief mates, and, as he sits on the deserted deck of the *Narcissus* after she has tied up at the dock in London, Baker muses about "all the successive ships to whom through many long years he had given the best of a seaman's care. And never a command in sight. Not once!" (p. 447). And we are at at as much of a loss to explain or understand the failure as is Baker.

But a common element appears in these two stories which may provide a clue. In both instances, the matter of luck has been raised, explicitly in Mahon's case and implicitly in Baker's. Both of these admirably qualified men have simply had no luck. They are, in effect, victims of circumstances and Conrad appears to be saying here that success in getting a command is as much a matter of chance as it is of desert or competence. Certainly the young captain in *The Shadow-Line* has all kinds of luck in finding himself the one qualified man available in Singapore when a new master is needed for the ship in Bangkok. Indeed, either Mahon or Baker, with their greater experience, would have been better qualified had they been available, and therein lies the rub. Similarly, in *Lord Jim,* Marlow accepts that chance can play a significant role in men's destinies. Marlow recognizes, for instance, that it was a lucky thing Jim had not loaded his revolver on his arrival in Patusan.

This emphasis on the role which luck or chance plays in men's destinies presents a new twist in our discussion and unearths an apparent contradiction in Conrad's vision of man. Elsewhere in *Lord Jim,* for instance, Marlow responds to Jim's somewhat naive belief that, after the *Patna* incident, he can begin again with a clean slate: "A clean slate, did he say? As if the initial word of each our destiny were not graven in imperishable characters upon the face of a rock!" (p. 113). With this pronouncement, Conrad is placing himself squarely in the ranks of the determinists who accept a world in which merit or luck or circumstances play no part. We appear to be left, on the one hand, with a Conrad who believes that happenstance can be a determinant in men's lives and, on the other hand, with a Conrad who accepts that fate, blind and disinterested, governs.

Conrad, however, would not have been aware of any contradiction, since, in his mind, luck and destiny were not mutually exclusive. Marlow says as much in *Lord Jim:* "There is a law, no doubt—and likewise a law regulates your luck in the throwing of dice" (p. 194). Thus, it is Mahon's and Baker's destiny to be unlucky, while in *The Shadow-Line,* it is the young captain's destiny to be lucky. He has, after all, left his post as chief mate of a perfectly satisfactory ship "for no reason on which a sensible person could put a finger" (p. 4), to go ashore at Singapore, as if, by this act, the new captain-to-be is fulfilling a predetermined pattern of which he is not himself aware.

Conrad devotes a rather lengthy section of *A Personal Record* to an accounting of the two lives he had led, his life at sea and his career as a creative artist. He finds that the two are not independent of each other, that in fact the one, the sea, provided the materials for much of the other, the writing. This is inevitable, says Conrad, echoing so many of his fellow literary craftsmen, since a writer can only write of what he himself has seen and experienced. Conrad quotes a favorite line from Anatole France in corroboration of this affinity between real and fictional life; writers must recognize, asserts this "most eloquent and just of French prose-writers," that "failing to hold our peace, we can only talk of ourselves" (p. 95).

In retrospect, it is evident that in stressing the unusual origins of so many of his seamen, in dwelling at length on the unfulfilled hopes and on the frustrations of those who fail to achieve command, and in sharing the elation of those few who succeed, Conrad has been, in large measure, talking of himself. A detailed study of Conrad's sea tales as autobiography—Conrad as Marlow, Conrad as the new captain in *The Shadow-Line,* the real and the fictional *Narcissus,* the Captain McWhirr whom Conrad knew and the Captain MacWhirr he invented—would demand more space than this study can allow. It will, however, be both possible and profitable here to demonstrate briefly how the fact of Conrad's career at sea significantly shaped not only the lives of his fictional seamen but also the very terms on which they live those lives.

With the frame of reference of Conrad's own years at sea in mind, it may be recognized that it is no accident that the large majority of Conrad's seamen are of the third category I have set up, the men who go to sea at an early age and acquire their mastery of the craft on countless decks and under innumerable sails. Conrad himself went to sea under just such conditions, at the age of eighteen, a bit late by the standards of the time, and he served his apprenticeship and his journeyman years on some twenty ships, if we count the S.S. *Roi de Belges,* the "two-penny-half-penny" steamboat of *Heart of Darkness.*

Similarly, with Conrad's own career in mind, it becomes easier to understand his pointing up the fact that so many of his seamen, far from being seamen at heart and by nature, are the products of the most unlikely and unpromising origins. It should be noted, of course, that Conrad is historically accurate here, since many commanders of fine merchant ships in Conrad's day *were* the sons of country parsons and Belfast greengrocers. But, at the same time, it is difficult to escape the feeling that Conrad was again talking of himself. For, what could be more implausible than that the young Teodor Korzeniowski, native of a landlocked middle European country and son of a Polish revolutionary

130   THE FELLOWSHIP OF THE CRAFT

and literary dilettante, should decide to become a seaman and, to push the implausible to the absolute limits, to decide, "If I was to be a seaman, then I would be a British seaman and no other" (*A Personal Record*, p. 119)? This is, indeed, the stuff which dreams are made on, and yet it came true, to the continuing wonderment of Thaddeus Bobrowski, Conrad's uncle and guardian, who, like MacWhirr's father, may have got used to the idea of having a seaman in the family but never really understood.

In like vein, Conrad's own career goes a long way toward accounting for his somewhat distorted view of the men who man ships, that is, his predilection for focusing his attention on the wardroom and the bridge and his preoccupation with the lives of the men in command and the crises which beset their lives. Within five years of setting out to be a seaman, Conrad had crossed that other shadow line which divides the deck and the bridge, becoming a third mate in 1880. Better than three-quarters of his twenty years at sea was thus spent in officers' country. The view from the bridge was the one Conrad knew best and understood best, and it is not surprising, therefore, that his fictional sea world is largely centered on that part of the ship where command is exercised and on the men who exercise it.

Finally, we may refer to Conrad's years at sea to understand better his obvious continuing fascination with all that has to do with commanding a ship, its demands, its conditions, and its rewards. Even more implausible than the Polish youth's proposing to become a British seaman is the truly astonishing fact that the young Korzeniowski, this most un-British of candidates for the fellowship of the craft, Slavic in temperament and features and speaking all of his life a heavily accented brand of English, succeeded against ludicrous odds and rose to the command of a British merchant ship. It is evident that throughout his later career, Conrad continued to be awed by the fact of having reached command status and elated by his extraordinary good fortune in having been, like the captain of *The Shadow-Line*, in the right place at the right time when opportunity came. This sense of awe and this feeling of elation show through in the sea stories whenever Conrad considers what it takes and what it means to command a ship. So too, having himself endured the trying years as a chief mate awaiting the largesse of fortune, Conrad's sympathies, as the tales make clear, are clearly with the Mahons and the Bakers, the worthy men who wait in vain.

Whatever their origins, whatever the path they take to the sea, and whatever their success or lack of it in attaining command, Conrad's seamen share one trait in common. They are, in the main, an exceptionally naive, unworldly, and even innocent group of men.

This high incidence of innocence among Conrad's seamen is not at all difficult to account for. They come, the majority of these men of the sea, from surroundings which are isolated and confining, either by fact of geography—Jim from a parsonage in Essex, Leggatt, the son of a parson in Norfolk, Allistoun from a family of sailors living at the northernmost tip of the British Isles—or from surroundings which are isolated and confining by reason of race or temperament. MacWhirr's ancestors, for instance, no doubt imported and maintained their dour, hard-working Calvinist ethic in crossing the Irish Sea to reside among the unbelievers of Northern Ireland. The predictable product of such restrictive and rarefied origins—such as Jim's and Leggatt's and Allistoun's and MacWhirr's—is the band of innocents that we find the seamen in Conrad to be. And, they carry their innocence and their ignorance with them aboard ship. The pattern, in almost all cases, is that just as these men reach a maturity sufficient to grasp something of the world and the men and women who inhabit it, they go to sea and are largely committed to the limited and limiting company of their fellow members of the craft.

Once the seaman has joined the fellowship, the opportunities for enlarging his knowledge and understanding of the world beyond the confines of the ship are extremely rare. His brief sojourns ashore are generally spent within the circle of his family, and, at best, he is exposed to only a few acquaintances beyond this circle, acquaintances who never really become friends, since the seaman does not have time to develop close relationships. Moreover, his sojourns are not only brief, they are also infrequent. Podmore, the *Narcissus*'s cook, is able to get home only once a year. Singleton, admittedly an extreme case, since he has nowhere to go anyway, has spent less than four of his forty-five years in the craft on shore. MacWhirr's children look upon the Captain of the *Nan-Shan* as a stranger who appears and disappears periodically, causing scarcely a ripple in the placid calm of family life which has evolved without him. Nor does the seaman's exposure to the ports and the peoples of the world broaden him as travel is alleged to do. We must keep in mind the judgment of the narrator of *Heart of Darkness* that most seamen are essentially stay-at-homes when abroad. Except for a brief and usually drunken foray ashore, the seaman is content to cling to the ship and has no interest in "the changing immensity of life" to be found at the foot of the ship's ladder.

Finally, in accounting for the extraordinary unworldliness of Conrad's seamen, something must be said of the special conditions that apply in the one world with which his seamen are genuinely familiar and in which they spend the greater part of their lives, the world of their seagoing homes, the world of the ships in which they serve. This is a highly artificial and an unusually sheltered world, a world isolated by the sea, not only from the mass of land but also from the many crises and calamities which beset the men who live on land. If the conventional metaphor of the ship as microcosm is true at all, it is true in the sense that the ship is a singular microcosm. As Conrad has more than once demonstrated, it is a highly disciplined, methodical, and orderly world of seldom varying routine in which each man plays a fixed part. Above all, it is an unequivocal world of orders given, orders received, and orders executed. There are few subtleties aboard ship, few surprises, and, except for purely professional matters, few occasions which call for niceties of judgment. The seaman who has been nurtured in this aseptic, rarefied atmosphere is ill equipped to cope with sophisticated human relationships or with a less than straightforward world in which appearance belies reality and shadow is often substituted for substance.

By and large, Conrad's seamen have a good deal to learn about themselves and about life as it is lived beyond the confines of the ship's rail. It is not surprising, therefore, that so many of Conrad's sea tales are stories of initiation, of the awakening of innocence.

We have already encountered and given some measure of

consideration to several of these stories in which innocence is initiated into awareness. In "Youth," for example, the young and ingenuous Marlow has his vistas broadened notably by the example of dedication to the ship given him by Captain Beard and also by his first sight of the Far East, a never-never land whose existence the twenty-year-old second mate had not contemplated even in his most exotic dreams. "The Secret Sharer" by its very title is a story of initiation—the new captain is introduced to the trials and the dilemmas of commanding a ship. In the end, he shares with Leggatt one of the great secrets of command—the willingness to dare and to risk. Like all of the inexperienced, he doubts himself and, like all of the uninitiated, he makes mistakes. For instance, in an effort to show himself a considerate and compassionate master, the new captain orders all hands to turn in, the gesture being the captain's way of recognizing the demanding day which the crew have undergone in making ready for sea. The captain volunteers to take the anchor watch himself, a clear violation of the custom of the sea and a disordering of the ship's routine. The captain later comes to regret his action when, alone on deck, he notices that the ship's rope side ladder has not been secured as it would have been had the anchor watch been set properly. Ironically, however, Conradian luck or fate, or the combination of the two, is on the captain's side and the oversight proves to be providential. It is the presence of the errant ladder which enables the swimmer, Leggatt, to come aboard ship.

In *The Shadow-Line,* Conrad himself makes the theme of initiation explicit. The Author's Note to the novel has this, the clearest statement of intent to be found in any of the introductions which Conrad provided to his works:

Primarily the aim of this piece of writing was the presentation of certain facts which certainly were associated with the change from youth, care-free and fervent, to the more self-conscious and more poignant period of maturer life. (p. viii)

As a consequence, the new captain of the story, after an initial period of doubt, masters the challenge both of the land (the fever which cripples his crew) and the sea (the calm which immobilizes his ship), brings his first command to port safely, and passes, himself, to that "period of maturer life" of which Conrad speaks.

Jukes, in *Typhoon,* is guilty of a youthful and innocent complacency, if not a form of *hubris,* in the airy letters which he addresses to his old chum and former shipmate, the second officer of the Atlantic liner, and his complacency extends to a reasonably satisfied view of himself and of his abilities. Like all of Conrad's innocents, Jukes has much to learn, but what is unusual about Jukes's case is the accelerated pace of his enlightenment. Within moments after the typhoon strikes, the bravado is gone and Jukes recognizes that what the *Nan-Shan* is faced with is "no joke." And, only a few moments after his initial awakening, as "a sudden lowering of the darkness came upon the night" (p. 39), Jukes's initiation is complete. He is, we are told, "uncritically glad to have his captain at hand" (p. 39).

The most comprehensive study of innocence and initiation in Conrad is to be seen in *The Nigger of the "Narcissus."* It is in this novel that we encounter perhaps the key statement of the unworldliness of the men who join the fellowship of the craft and follow the sea. Conrad begins by depicting Singleton as a "sixty-year-old-child" of the sea, but the charge of innocence is not confined to Singleton. The old sailor becomes, in fact, a type for all the seamen who went before the mast in Conrad's time, a simpler and, therefore, a better time, we are given to understand. Of these men, the many seamen whom he knew in his twenty years at sea, Conrad remarks:

Their generation lived inarticulate and indispensable, without knowing the sweetness of affections or the refuge of a home—and died free from the dark menace of a narrow grave. They were the everlasting children of the mysterious sea. Their successors are the grown-up children of a discontented earth. They are less naughty, but less innocent. (p. 313)

But Conrad does not ask us to accept the childlike nature of the seaman on the basis of some generalized statements and arbitrary pronouncements, however knowledgeable they may be. Innocence abounds on the *Narcissus* and Conrad renders it dramatically and visually.

There is, for instance, the splendid vignette early in the tale of Singleton sitting apart on deck and laboriously working his way through the pages of *Pelham* and, no doubt, naively accepting Bulwer-Lytton's imagined world for the real world, of which Singleton knows so little. The narrator is prompted to wonder at the novel's mysterious appeal for such as Singleton and to speculate on the ideas that these "polished and so curiously insincere sentences awaken in the simple minds of the big children who people those dark and wandering places of the earth" (p. 295).

By way of further illustration of the innocence which prevails aboard the *Narcissus,* one might cite the ludicrous symposium held on deck among some of the most unpolished members of the crew on the question of how a gentleman may be recognized. It is perhaps enough that such as these should be engaged in so irrelevant a discussion aboard a sailing vessel hundreds of miles at sea, but Knowles's assertion that the gentleman may be detected by the thinness of the seat of his trousers "from constant sitting down in offices" (p. 320) is clear evidence that we are in the midst of simple hearts and minds. And even in matters of the sea, where they do have some expertise, the crew of the *Narcissus* have much to learn. Long before the storm has peaked, they are convinced "it can blow no harder" (p. 341), and Baker and Creighton have their hands full keeping the men at work getting ready for the full force of the gale which the officers' greater experience or greater understanding tell them is yet to come.

Singleton is fated to go on believing in Bulwer-Lytton's never-never land, and the crew are destined never to be enlightened on the hallmarks of a gentleman. But, during the course of the voyage from Bombay to London, both the patriarch of the sea and the men of the *Narcissus*'s forecastle undergo another and far more profound initiation.

Singleton, notably, does not share the crew's delusion that they can save Jimmy Wait and cheat death. The ancient mariner has seen death many times during his long years at sea and he recognizes a dying man when he sees one. He pronounces that Jimmy is doomed and that he will die within sight of land. But, it becomes evident that Singleton's wisdom is incomplete or is, at least, limited. Singleton has accepted death only in the abstract, and it is not until he collapses after his thirty-hour stint at the wheel that the concrete fact of his own mortality is thrust upon him. For the first time, Singleton must deal with the idea that even his "body of an old athlete" must weaken and die. The revelation is shattering for the stolid Singleton and, like all sudden insights into the self, it is difficult for him to accept:

He brooded alone more than ever, in an impenetrable silence and with a saddened face. . . . He had never given a thought to his mortal self. He lived unscathed, as though he had been indestructible, surrendering to all the temptations, weathering many gales. He had panted in sunshine, shivered in the cold; suffered hunger, thirst, debauch; passed through many trials—known all the furies. Old! It seemed to him he was broken at last. (p. 382)

It is unlikely that Singleton ever fully accepts, since it needs a rare spirit to accept the fact of one's own mortality. In time, however, he is able to acquiesce, and the narrator later writes of the ship moving out of the storm, carrying "Singleton's completed wisdom" (p. 383).

The crew of the *Narcissus,* with two exceptions, are the victims of a grand-scale delusion whose proportions display the singular innocence of the victims. They are convinced that they can save Jimmy Wait and cheat death, not only for this time but for all time. Singleton is spared this particular madness. The narrator too largely divorces himself from the crew's mania, but ultimately, even the narrator's position becomes ambiguous. In general, he reveals himself as a cut above his shipmates in his knowledge of the world and the roles which men play in it, and he sees the crew's obsession for the chimera that it is. At times, however, the narrator seems to get caught up in the prevailing delirium and champions the crew in their impossible quest. (He is one of the five, for instance, who rescue Jimmy from the capsized deck-house.) It is this ambivalence of attitude that accounts for the narrator's strange alternation between the third person, "they," and the first person, "we," in speaking of the crew, a point that has troubled many of Conrad's critics.

For the rest of the *Narcissus*'s crew, however, the saving of Jimmy Wait becomes a fixed resolve, wherein their unworldliness stands revealed in their passion for the hopeless cause and their apparent readiness to believe the impossible. Quite simply, they are prepared to believe that they can spare Jimmy Wait from death merely by willing him not to die. "We wanted," says the narrator, positioning himself with the crew for the moment, "to keep him alive till home—to the end of the voyage" (p. 422), and their efforts on this behalf take many forms. There is, for instance, the rescue of Jimmy during the storm, and here, literally, it is by their efforts that Jimmy is kept alive. After the rescue, the boatswain puts their grand design into explicit terms. In response to Mr. Baker's demand to know what the five who rescue Jimmy are up to, the boatswain replies, "We are trying to keep life in that poor devil" (pp. 363–64). Podmore, the cook, visits Jimmy at night bringing him material (a pot of cold tea sweetened with white sugar) and spiritual sustenance; Belfast becomes Jimmy's self-appointed nurse and spends "every moment of his spare time" (p. 421) in Jimmy's makeshift sick bay; one by one the rest of the crew come to Jimmy's cabin, and their motive is to add their bit of strength to the collective effort to preserve Jimmy:

They spoke in clear voices, pronounced cheerful words, repeated old jokes, listened to him; and each, going out, seemed to leave behind a little of his own vitality, surrender some of his own strength, renew the assurance of life—the indestructible thing!
(pp. 428–29)

But the crew's concern is not without self-interest. For, in their innocence, what they propose to do is nothing less than to outface death and, by saving Jimmy, save themselves. Singleton recognizes, perhaps from the beginning, the extraordinary emphasis which the crew place on sustaining Jimmy. "You can't help him; die he must" (p. 411), he assures them, and in the next breath he adds, "You can't help yourselves" (p. 412).

When Jimmy dies, the crew are exposed for the group of

innocents that they really are and their grand obsession for the pitiable folly that it really is. The disillusionment is an immense shock and one for which they are totally unprepared:

> Jimmy's death, after all, came as a tremendous surprise. We did not know till then how much faith we had put in his delusions. We had taken his chances of life so much at his own valuation that his death, like the death of an old belief, shook the foundations of our society. (p. 436)

To give the crew their just due, however, recognition of their delusion and a measure of acceptance are arrived at fairly speedily; certainly, awareness comes much more rapidly and is more complete than in Singleton's case. "It was just common foolishness," they conclude, "a silly and ineffectual meddling with issues of majestic import" (p. 437).

At the close of the novel, the narrator, having received his final pay, stands apart once more from his shipmates and addresses them, figuratively: "Haven't we, together and upon the immortal sea, wrung out a meaning from our sinful lives?" (p. 453). There are a number of issues involved in the narrator's use of "meaning," but surely one of them is that the crew have been initiated to a salient fact of life, which is the fact of death. The crew have learned that all men, and indeed all ships, are fated to die, since, as the narrator has just pronounced and as we have been reminded again and again in the course of *The Nigger of the "Narcissus,"* only the sea is immortal.

In this brief and incomplete consideration of innocence and initiation aboard Conrad's ships, one striking point has come to light. In every case of enlightenment and understanding, the initiation has taken place only when the ship is subjected to some extraordinary set of conditions or circumstances or when some foreign element is introduced which seems to trigger the process of initiation. In "Youth," for example, it is the exception to the norm, the fire at sea, which enables the young Marlow to see, through the example of Beard, what fidelity to the ship and to the craft is all about. In "The Secret Sharer," it is the unexpected appearance of Leggatt that provides the new captain with the initial test of his capacity for command. In the case of the captain of *The Shadow-Line,* two catalysts, both out of the ordinary, prompt his reaching a new maturity—the fever which has laid hold of his men and the exceptional atmospheric conditions which have becalmed his ship. In *Typhoon,* it is the emergency created by the hurricane which brings Jukes to a better understanding of his strengths and his weaknesses. And aboard the *Narcissus,* it is the storm, in Singleton's case, and the presence of Jimmy Wait, in the case of the crew, which bring the old sailor and the crew, respectively, to a recognition of their common and inevitable mortality. The conclusion to be inferred from all of these instances is in accord with the thesis proposed above: under normal circumstances, the ship is a limited and insulated community which, by cutting men off from the main stream of life, preserves their innocence. Only when the ship or its men are under stress or are touched by influences beyond the normal and the everyday does the enlightenment of innocence take place.

In Charlie Marlow, we appear to have the exception among Conrad's children of the sea. Here, at least and at last, we have a Conradian seaman who has long since put his innocence behind him and who has long since given over whatever illusions he may have once had—about himself, about the world, and about the fellow creatures with whom he shares a foothold on the planet. After all, as we have been unequivocally informed in *Heart of Darkness,* Marlow is different from all other seamen. He is, in fact, unique among seamen in several ways, all of them touching upon his greater awareness and understanding. First of all, Marlow is unique in that he is curious, about people and places and manners and customs and mores and motives, in sum, about all life. Not for him is the "sedentary life" led by the "stay-at-home" order of seamen whose horizons are defined by the forecastle and the deck, whether at sea or in port. Marlow's residence is the world, and he is as much at home on land as at sea. He is, by the particular designation of the narrator of *Heart of Darkness,* a "wanderer," and his wanderings at sea and his excursions ashore have given him a significant knowledge of "the foreign shores, the foreign faces, the changing immensity of life" (*Heart of Darkness,* p. 5).

Marlow is unique, too, in his accessibility—or perhaps vulnerability would be the better term. He has the curious facility for finding himself right smack in the path of experience and in the center of events. Although this facility has enlarged Marlow's vistas appreciably, he professes to find it a nuisance at times, and in *Lord Jim* he complains:

> I am willing to believe each of us has a guardian angel, if you fellows will concede to me that each of us has a familiar devil as well. . . . I know I have him—the devil, I mean. . . . He is there right enough, and, being malicious, he lets me in for that kind of thing. What kind of thing, you ask? . . . the kind of thing that by devious, unexpected, truly diabolical ways causes me to run up against men with soft spots, with hard spots, with hidden plague spots, by Jove! and loosens their tongues at the sight of me for their infernal confidences. . . . And what I have done to be thus favored I want to know. (p. 21)

But Marlow's pique must be taken at a good deal less than face value, for it is his penchant for being highly visible which makes him vulnerable, and it is unlikely that Marlow would, or could, be content with a supernumerary's role.

Finally, Marlow is unique in that he exhibits a sentience that is uncommon, if not totally rare, among Conrad's seamen. Despite his disclaimers that he never "sees" Jim clearly or his lamentations that he is not able to "see" Kurtz as clearly as he should, Marlow's vision is, on the whole, excellent. In "Youth," for instance, he is able to see, in retrospect, his own innocence and naivete and, at the same time, to regret their passing. Marlow sees the subtleties and the ironies of Jim's situation with great clarity, and he sees immediately the speciousness and the hypocrisy of the "Pilgrims of Progress" whom he encounters in the Congo.

And yet, for all his awareness, his wide experience, his sensitivity and his perception, Marlow is still capable of learning. And, indeed, the learning process does go on in the sea stories. What, for example, is *Heart of Darkness* if it is not a story of initiation? Marlow certainly is quite aware that his journey into the heart of darkness has enlarged and enlightened him. Looking back at himself, pre-Congo, Marlow is able to recognize and to be amused by his own innocence as he walked down the Strand and was arrested by the serpent-shaped map of the Congo in the shop window. "It fascinated me," says Marlow, "as a snake would a bird—a silly little bird" (p. 8), and the metaphor Marlow employs is quite just, suggesting, as it does, the confrontation of innocence and evil. At the same time, the highly dramatic terms in which the metaphor is couched do double duty, hinting with the bird, on the one hand, at Marlow's earlier utter helplessness in the face of an unknown danger and with the snake, on the other hand, at his later recognition of the extent of that danger. Later, on his return from the Congo, Marlow again walks the streets of a city, this time the city that always makes Marlow think of "a whited sepulchre" (p. 9), and he is both appalled and exasperated by the callousness of the innocents who pass him by, the innocents who have not shared his experience and his initiation in the Congo. "They were intruders," Marlow affirms, "whose knowledge of life was to me an irritating pretence, because I felt so sure they could not possibly know the things I knew"; and he finds their everyday bearing "like the outrageous flauntings of folly in the face of a danger it is unable to comprehend" (p. 72).

What are these things that Marlow now knows that have wrought this remarkable transformation and made of the bird-like innocent a sage and oracle who is qualified to pass judgment on half the city of Brussels? They are several. On the more obvious level, Marlow has been enlarged and enlightened by his encounter with the "flabby, pretending, weak-eyed devil of a rapacious and pitiless folly" (p. 17), as Marlow calls it—the great sham, in other words, being perpetrated in the Congo by the company in the name of progress and civilization. Marlow has also learned something of the therapeutic nature of work. Keeping the "tin pot" steamship afloat has given him a chance, as he puts it, to find himself—"Your own reality—for yourself, not for others—what no other man can ever know" (p. 29). And the long weeks spent restoring his command have provided Marlow with an even more telling insight. Stripped of the nonessentials, life, Marlow discovers, can resolve itself into so simple a matter as the need for rivets, and placing those rivets properly can be the means of survival and salvation. Because of the steamboat and because of the rivets, Marlow emerges from the jungle, tainted, but not seriously compromised by the touch of evil.

Chiefly, however, and this is the immense secret which Marlow carries about with him through the streets of Brussels, the jungle has opened Marlow's eyes to the stunning discovery that there are, in fact, two hearts of darkness: the external and physical darkness which exists in the Congo and the internal and spiritual darkness which lies in the soul of man. What Marlow could tell the passersby, if he would, and what he must bite his tongue to keep from telling Kurtz's Intended, is his recognition of how near to the surface this latter darkness is and how thin and fragile is the veneer of civilization which covers it. This knowledge Marlow has come by through a series of initiations—through his attempts to cope with the ruined Kurtz and his maddened soul, through his exposure to the triumphant lunacy which reigns unchecked in the Congo, and, most importantly, through his own alarming response to the sound of the drums he heard on the river which spoke to him from the earliest and darkest ages.

There remain to be considered the two most intriguing and most controversial of Conrad's innocents of the sea, Jim and Tom Lingard.

It is unlikely that any reader of *Lord Jim* would take issue with the proposition that Jim is probably the most complete of Conrad's innocents. Jim's lack of worldliness is, in fact, a kind of ground root impression which most readers bring away from the novel without ever really knowing why they feel this way, except, perhaps, that there is a predisposition to equate the term "romantic," which is several times applied to Jim, with the term "innocent." Over and above this facile association, however, Jim as innocent receives considerable stress in the novel, although this motif tends to be subsumed under the weight of the main thrust of the story, which is directed toward establishing and fixing, in the reader's mind, Jim's hopeless romanticism.

In assaying Jim's innocence, there are several details of his physical appearance, for instance, which deserve more than casual consideration. *Lord Jim* opens with a description of Jim, and from it Jim emerges as a man to be reckoned with. He was, we are told,

. . . an inch, perhaps two, under six feet, powerfully built, and he advanced straight at you with a slight stoop of the shoulders, head forward, and a fixed from-under stare which made you think of a charging bull. (p. 3)

In all, this is the demeanor of a man who is very much sure of himself, even to the point of some combativeness. But Jim's prepossessing air is belied later when Marlow mentions the most striking feature of Jim's makeup, a feature which has obviously engaged Marlow's close attention, since he refers to it on at least three occasions; Jim has, by Marlow's testimony, astonishingly "clear, blue eyes" (p. 46). Moreover, and here we are again indebted to Marlow's perceptiveness, Jim's eyes have the peculiar faculty of darkening noticeably whenever he is under stress or excited, and the clear implication which Marlow would convey to us is that Jim flushes and blushes easily.

In a like vein, it is impossible to overlook the symbolic import of Jim's dress. Jim's characteristic attire is impressed on the reader's consciousness in the opening paragraph of the novel. He is "spotlessly neat, apparelled in immaculate white from shoes to hat" (p. 3), and, although we are not told so explicitly, presumably this was also Jim's attire when his and Marlow's eyes first met in the courtroom during the proceedings of the Board of Inquiry into the *Patna* affair. In any event, it *is* Jim's attire when Marlow gets his last glimpse of Jim from the rail of the schooner which takes Marlow from Patusan. Jim stands on the beach until the ship disappears from sight, and Marlow reports the scene in some of Conrad's most moving and most symbol-laden prose:

He was white from head to foot, and remained persistently visible with the stronghold of the night at his back. . . . For me that white figure in the stillness of coast and sea seemed to stand at the heart of a vast enigma. The twilight was ebbing fast from the sky above his head, the strip of sand had sunk already under his feet, he himself appeared no bigger than a child—then only a speck, a tiny white speck, that seemed to catch all the light left in a darkened world. . . . And, suddenly, I lost him. . . . (p. 204)

So too, Jim is garbed in white during the decisive confrontation with Gentleman Brown across the creek in Patusan. And it is again difficult to escape the larger meaning with which Conrad has imbued this meeting, the classic encounter of good (or innocence, in Jim's case) and evil, each holding his own ground on one bank of the creek with the neutral zone of the creek's waters dividing them. Brown's appearance, too, is significant. In contrast to the immaculate and impeccable Jim, Brown is positively grubby "in a checked flannel shirt with sleeves cut off at the elbows, grey bearded, with a sunken, sun-blackened face" (p. 231).

Moreover, in marshalling the evidence of Jim's innocence to be found in the text, some attention must be given to the impression which Jim makes on the people he encounters. In the midst of the many tentative judgments which Marlow passes on Jim, for instance, there is one evaluation which remains a constant. Marlow is continually struck by Jim's boyishness, and he consistently employs terms such as "youngster," "boy," "youth," "childlike" in speaking of Jim. In his last view of Jim, he appears, to Marlow's eyes, "no bigger than a child" (p. 204); at one point, Conrad very nearly lets his persona become a bit heavy-handed, as Marlow refers to Jim's "blue, boyish eyes" (p. 48). The wise Stein, to whom even the worldly and urbane Marlow defers, sums up Marlow's verbal description of Jim by observing, "Yes; he is young," and Stein concurs with Marlow's epigrammatic observation that Jim is "the youngest human being now in existence" (p. 134).

But, it is not only to Jim's friends that his innocence is evident; to his detriment and his ultimate harm, the weakness is also detected by Jim's enemies. Cornelius, for example, with the acute perception sometimes given to the depraved, dismisses Jim as "no more than a little child" (p. 199), and it is one of the sad facts of Jim's world that the wicked, in Chester's phrase, "see things exactly as they are" much more readily than do the virtuous. Gentleman Brown is gifted with this same perverse clarity of vision and was able to see "directly I set my eyes on him" what sort of "fool" Jim was (p. 209); given the inspired way in which

Brown manipulates Jim, he might very well have echoed Cornelius and called Jim "child" instead of "fool".

But Conrad does not expect the reader to accept Jim as innocent solely on the basis of the labels and tags applied to him
or the judgments passed on him by his fellow characters in the
novel. Rather, Jim's innocence is amply demonstrated on a number of occasions. When Marlow offers to write to his friend, the
owner of the rice mill, on Jim's behalf, Jim's enthusiasm and his
gratitude are childishly excessive. He veritably gushes, and the
highly sensitive Marlow finds the episode painful:

"You are a brick!" he cried next in a muffled voice. . . . "Why!
this is what I—you—I . . . I would be a brute now if I. . . ."
"That's all right," I said. I was almost alarmed by this display of
feeling, through which pierced a strange elation. I had pulled the
string accidentally, as it were; I did not fully understand the working of the toy. "I must go now," he said. "Jove! You *have* helped
me. Can't sit still. The very thing. . . ." He looked at me with
puzzled admiration. "The very thing. . . ." (p. 112)

Similarly, Jim contemplates his exile on Patusan with all the zest
and excitement of a glorious, romantic adventure. Marlow, on
the other hand, has, somewhat cynically, already recognized the
removal to Patusan as the fulfillment of Brierly's suggestion that
Jim be allowed to "creep twenty feet underground and stay there"
(p. 41). Marlow is prepared to be amused by Jim's posturings,
but he finds himself, instead, appalled by the depth of naivete
which they reveal:

He impressed, almost frightened me with his elated rattle. He was
voluble like a youngster on the eve of a long holiday with a prospect
of delightful scrapes, and such an attitude of mind in a grown man
and in this connection had in it something phenomenal, a little
mad, dangerous, unsafe. (p. 143)

In Tom Lingard, we encounter an innocent of almost equal
proportions. For all his knowledge of ships and hidden channels
and dangerous reefs and for all the universal acceptance he enjoys as "King of the Sea," Lingard is largely untutored in many
other areas and in many other respects. It is, in fact, this very
lack of sophistication in Lingard that the world-weary and jaded

Mrs. Travers finds so attractive. Consider, for instance, the following exchange, in which Lingard tells Mrs. Travers of an opera he had once seen in Melbourne while on a holiday spree from the gold mines of the outback:

". . . that story with music I am telling you of, Mrs. Travers, was not a tale for children. I assure you that of the few shows I have seen that one was the most real to me. More real than anything in life."

Mrs. Travers, remembering the fatal inanity of most opera librettos, was touched by these words as if there had been something pathetic in this readiness of response. . . . "I suppose you forgot yourself in that story, whatever it was," she remarked in a detached tone.

"Yes, it carried me away. But I suppose you know the feeling."

(*The Rescue,* p. 301)

To which Mrs. Travers replies, "No." And indeed, there is something pathetic, yet apparently appealing to Mrs. Travers, in Lingard's childlike enthusiasm for what was undoubtedly a second-rate performance by a second-rate company.

But Lingard's uncomplicated view of the great world beyond the confines of the brig *Lightning* is harmless enough. What is not so innocuous, however, what is, in fact, critical and ultimately fatal is Lingard's innocent belief in his own infallibility and invulnerability. As Lingard tells her of his plan to play kingmaker and reestablish Hassim as ruler of the Wajos, even the normally skeptical Mrs. Travers is carried away by his fire and his enthusiasm:

What of it that the narrator was only a roving seaman; the kingdom of the jungle, the men of the forest, the lives obscure! That simple soul was possessed by the greatness of the idea; there was nothing sordid in its flaming impulses. When she once understood that, the story appealed to the audacity of her thoughts, and she became so charmed with what she heard that she forgot where she was.

(pp. 162–63)

Both Mrs. Travers and Lingard are, of course, caught up by the romance of it all, until the plan assumes the deceptive reality of the opera Lingard had seen in Melbourne and Lingard, especially, loses sight of what *can* be in his obsession with what *should* be.

If we look back over the more prominent cases of innocence initiated which take place aboard Conrad's ships, a significant pattern may be observed. In each instance, the initiate undergoes a period of doubt during the course of the initiation, and this time of questioning is extremely salutary; indeed, it would appear to be a condition of successful initiation. The young captain in "The Secret Sharer," for instance, doubts his capacity for command, as does the new master in *The Shadow-Line*. Singleton's "completed wisdom" is to be found largely in his new awareness of his own limitations, a truth he arrives at only after a period of misgiving during which Singleton questions, perhaps for the first time, his abilities and capabilities. Marlow doubts at several junctures in *Heart of Darkness*. For example, shortly after his first exposure to the lunatic asylum which is the Congo, Marlow wonders if the mental changes of which the doctor in Brussels who took his cranial measurements warned are not, in fact, already taking place. And others among Conrad's initiates are given to healthy questioning.

It is otherwise with Jim and Lingard. Jim never does doubt, while Lingard pauses to reflect and take stock only after it is already too late. And it is not that either of the two lacks sufficient reason or sufficient opportunity to doubt. For instance, Jim surely should have paid some heed to the preliminary warning of his shortcomings which he receives when he funks during the crisis on the training ship. Instead, Jim rationalizes that this was not a proper trial, that he is being spared for greater things. This same proclivity for rationalization may be seen in the *Patna* incident. To Marlow's continuing annoyance, Jim persists in seeing the episode as a chance missed, rather than as a test failed. It is true, of course, that Jim pays lip service to the situation as it really is in standing trial before the Board of Inquiry. But the trial ultimately brings about more harm than good. Jim interprets the court's verdict as a receipt marked "Paid in Full," which frees him to indulge his fatal imagination in his own fanciful version of the *Patna* affair. So, too, on Patusan, Jim is given to easy certainty when healthly doubt is called for. Jim is convinced that he has mastered his own fate, and in this conviction he closes his ears to any voices but his own. There are the voices of Jewell and

Dain Waris, for instance, who urge him to meet force with force, and Tamb' Itam, for whom coping with Gentleman Brown is no more than "the taking of another hill" (p. 237). And they certainly have a right to be heard, since their lives are at stake too. Liar and braggart though he may be, Brown is right about one thing; Jim is a "fool," for being so readily duped by Brown's blandishments and for taking the lives of so many people on his own compromised head. It follows that I do not see Jim's death as being in any way heroic. Rather, it is the desperate act of an essentially decent man who has simply run out of options.

In similar fashion, there are several instances in Tom Lingard's flamboyant career when he might have, or should have, had occasion to question and to doubt. As a case in point, had Lingard not been so engrossed in shaping the world to suit his own design, he might have questioned his judgment in entrusting the welfare of the settlement at Sambir and of his adopted Malay daughter to the incompetent Almayer, a man utterly bankrupt of material and spiritual resources. This same lack of judgment is to be seen in Lingard's insistence on introducing into the community at Sambir the outcast, Willems, who has already failed miserably the two earlier opportunities Lingard has given him. Even the normally dense Almayer protests Lingard's action, but Lingard is adamant and the results, predictably, are disastrous. Finally, it is not unreasonable to expect that Lingard should have had some doubts about the feasibility of what he proposes to do in *The Rescue*. Not content with being a king himself, Lingard would create a king, single-handedly restoring Hassim to the throne and single-handedly determining the destinies of the Wajo people. It is not until chance, a factor with which Lingard fails to reckon, shatters his plans that Lingard is able to see the extent of his folly.

The trouble with Jim and with Lingard is that both men are egotists of considerable magnitude, and this overweening sense of self is their common tragic flaw. Embued as Jim and Lingard are with a conviction of their superiority, they feel no need for the doubts and fears, the appraisals and reappraisals which are the lot of common men. Indeed, any attempt on their part to take stock would be futile, since, in their spiritual blindness, neither of the two men is able to see himself as he is, his situation as it is, or the world as it is. Jim, for instance, despite the clear, although unspoken, message of the failure on the training ship and of the debacle aboard the *Patna,* remains unshaken in his conviction that he is destined to perform heroics on the scale set forth by the "course of light holiday literature." He is equally convinced that he is destined to view life from some such elevated perspective as that afforded him when he stood in the crow's nest of the training ship and saw the world below him, at his feet. (I maintain that Jim's conviction remains unshaken, unless the note which he started at the Fort on Patusan, which begins, "An awful thing has happened" [p. 207], is the first glimmering of anagnorisis.)

Lingard has an equally grandiose and distorted view of himself. He has, in effect, come to believe in his own legend that, as the Rajah Laut, "the King of the Sea," he is invincible and infallible and that all which his hands touch will, perforce, prosper and thrive. And in *The Rescue,* it is only when everyone who has trusted him has been killed, largely through his mismanagement, that Lingard is willing, or able, to consider the role which his unfettered ego has played in the disaster.

There is surely a strain of arrogance intermixed with Jim's innocence when he proclaims to Marlow at virtually their last meeting that "nothing can touch me" (p. 203). If my chronology is correct, Jim's assertion of his impregnability precedes the coming of Gentleman Brown by a matter of a few months at the most. But the most explicit and most telling statement of Jim's egotism is uttered, as might be expected, by Marlow. Marlow closes his letter detailing the terminal events on Patusan with a final attempt to "see" Jim: "We can see him, an obscure conqueror of fame, tearing himself out of the arms of a jealous love at the sign, at the call of his exalted egoism" (p. 253). Marlow's words gain emphasis, of course, coming where they do, at the end of the novel, as Marlow considers Jim for the last time and prepares, as best he can, to put the episode behind him. The passage represents the closest Marlow will ever come to a final judgment on Jim. As such, one may assume that Marlow speaks with considerable care, and thus the weight that he quite

clearly assigns to Jim's "exalted egoism" in his summing up of
Jim is inescapable.

Lingard's arrogance and self-assurance would almost be
comic, were they not also frightening in their capacity for doing
harm. For instance, in *An Outcast of the Islands,* Lingard
boasts of the private world he has created at Sambir, on the
River Pantai, and the passage is nearly overwhelmed by his
persistent use of the personal pronoun:

> "I have my own trading post in the place. Almayer is my partner.
> You knew him when he was at Hudigs'. Oh, he lives there as
> happy as a king. D'ye see, I have them all in my pocket. The rajah
> is an old friend of mine. My word is law—and I am the only trader."
> (p. 43)

In all of this, there is no hint of any awareness on Lingard's
part that he has effected a grand misalliance in arranging the
marriage of convenience between Almayer and the Malayan
girl who survived one of Lingard's more adventurous forays. Nor
is there any hint of misgivings about the wisdom of placing the
stolid, unimaginative Almayer in charge of the trading post. In
view of the intricate alliances and feuds among the native fac-
tions, the success of the trading mission at Sambir calls for the
nicest tact and the most delicate handling, and it is precisely in
both of these talents that Almayer is chiefly deficient.

Lingard's arrogance is never more evident and never more
unnerving than in the following passage, also from *An Outcast
of the Islands,* in which we eavesdrop on a mind so filled with
a sense of the self that egotism very nearly spills over into ego-
mania. Lingard is again speaking of Sambir:

> . . . knowing nothing of Arcadia—he dreamed of Arcadian happi-
> ness for that little corner of the world which he loved to think
> all his own. His deep-seated and immovable conviction that only
> he—he, Lingard—knew what was good for them was characteristic
> of him, and, after all, not so very far wrong. He would make them
> happy whether or no, he said, and he meant it. (p. 200)

Finally, there is the passage from *The Rescue* in which
Lingard mentally turns over his plans for Hassim's return to the

throne. Noble as Lingard's motives may be and stirring as his words strike the listener, there is, in his vision of the future of the Wajo people, a strong sense of the importance, if not to say centrality, of the presence of Tom Lingard for the success of the undertaking:

For two years, Lingard, who had thrown himself body and soul into the great enterprise, had lived in the long intoxication of slowly preparing success. No thought of failure had crossed his mind, and no price appeared too heavy to pay for such a magnificent achievement. . . . When at the conclusion of some long talk with Hassim . . . he lifted his big arm and shaking his fist above his head, shouted: "We will stir them up. We will wake up the country!" he was, without knowing it in the least, making a complete confession of the idealism hidden under the simplicity of his strength. He would wake up the country! That was the fundamental and unconscious emotion on which were engrafted his need of action, the primitive sense of what was due to justice . . . the proud conviction that of all the men in the world, in his world, he alone had the means and the pluck "to lift up the big end" of such an adventure. (p. 106)

CHAPTER SIX

FELLOWSHIP OF THE CRAFT

We have come full circle. We began with Tom Lingard and we end with Tom Lingard. And we end with a Tom Lingard who—despite his appellation, "the King of the Sea," despite his immense professional skill and daring, and despite his brave assertion, with which this book opened, that the sea is his and all seamen's proper habitat—has not learned, or, at least, has not fully understood, two cardinal truths which Joseph Conrad educed from his early calling as a seaman: the craft is greater than any one of its members; no seaman, however worthy, is "at home" at sea. Rather, he is there by the sea's sufferance, and only through a continuing awareness of this dispensation, every working hour, every waking hour, is he able to fulfill the seaman's sole mission, which is "to keep ships' keels off the ground."

In turn, we have arrived at some truths concerning Conrad and ships and seamen and the sea which go far toward answering the questions and testing the generalizations evoked at the beginning of this book.

For example, on the face of the evidence, both explicit and implicit, it appears that Conrad was sufficiently attached to the land to share the seaman's traditional longing for a safe port after a perilous passage. Witness, for instance, Conrad's almost lyrical description of Landfall and Departure—especially Landfall—in *The Mirror of the Sea* and Captain Allistoun's vision of retirement "far in the country—out of sight of the sea." At the same time, the evidence also reveals that Conrad was very much aware of the debilitating effect, on both men and ships, of prolonged association with the land. Witness, for instance,

152

Singleton's gaucherie when ashore and the heavy drinking of the admirable Mr. B—, "the best of second mates," while in port, and the symbolic death of the *Narcissus* as it docks in London and the taint which the unnamed ship in *The Shadow-Line* has carried with it to sea as a legacy from the land.

This ambivalence is even more evident and more pronounced when we turn to Conrad's attitude toward the sea. *Odi et amo,* Conrad says, is the reasonable, the sensible, the only viable attitude toward the sea, and both in his own voice and in the voices of his fictional narrators, he returns to this theme many times and in many places. For Conrad and for the seamen who man his imagined ships on their imagined voyages, the glamor, the romance, the inescapable appeal of the sea comes through in passage after passage, but so too does an ever-present sense of the treachery, the violence, the hatefulness of what has always been and will always be a cruel and implacable sea. Conrad would dismiss, with some impatience, Tom Lingard's expansive pronouncement that the sea is the only place for an honest man. Purity of heart and motives simply won't do in coping with an adversary endowed with the guile of which the sea is capable. Only a prudent, a cautious, a wary, and an honest man can hope to survive. Conrad has put it best: "He . . . who putting his trust in the friendship of the sea, neglects the strength and cunning of his right hand, is a fool!"

If Conrad reserved his wholehearted affection for anything, it was not for the sea but rather for ships, and one wonders if this is not true of all men who go to sea. When, for instance, a seaman, be he a professional, like Conrad, or a weekend sailor, speaks of his love of the sea, doesn't he really mean his love of "the faithful servants," as Conrad called them, who take him to sea? In any event, the point need not be labored here. Singleton has said it all, "Ships are all right," and Conrad has concurred, "No ship is wholly bad," not even the noisy, unwieldy and evil-smelling steamships which, near the end of Conrad's career as a seaman, were just beginning to befoul the pristine seas of the world. But the worthiest ships of all, it becomes clear from reading Conrad's pages, were the great and graceful "birds" of the sea, the clipper ships of the 1870s and 1880s, the ships which Conrad knew and viewed with increasing affection as they passed, rather suddenly, into the pages of history.

Toward the craft, Conrad's attitude is again unequivocal. The craft, for Conrad, is among the noblest of man's pursuits; and to be a worthy member of the fellowship of the craft, among the noblest of man's aspirations. This is in direct contrast to Conrad's views about writing, for example, over which he agonized and at which he seldom exulted. Invariably, he was troubled by the persistent fear that what he had wrought had come by a lucky chance and labored under the continuing conviction that his latest book would, perforce, be his last.

Curiously enough, given the many times that the phrase has been used in this book, we have not yet arrived at a working definition of "the fellowship of the craft" and, more important, at a summary statement of the qualifications of a member in good standing of the fellowship. The neglect has not been intentional; as employed by Conrad, the terms "the fellowship" and "the craft" do not readily render themselves up; but, we can try.

Conrad and Marlow are jointly responsible for coining the phrase "the fellowship of the craft"; Conrad uses it in *The Mirror of the Sea,* and he is echoed by Marlow in "Youth." But, having said the words, both seem to assume a certain omniscience on the part of the reader; as we have noted in chapter 4, both indulge in considerable shuffling about and waffling in talking about "the fellowship" and "the craft," and they never really get down to terms. In *Lord Jim,* for example, Marlow natters away enigmatically about "the craft" and especially about what he calls its "little mysteries." A careful reading of Conrad reveals that these "mysteries" are nothing more than those fixed guiding principles, those elementary rules of conduct to which all worthy seamen subscribe. And to be worthy, a seaman must exhibit, preeminently, three attributes: first he must be faithful —the note of fidelity or its variant, trust, is struck again and again in Conrad's works until one has the distinct feeling that "faithful" must have been Conrad's most treasured epithet and one which he did not bestow gratuitously; second, the proper seaman must be a highly disciplined man, both within and without, and with an immense capacity for getting on with the work; finally, he must always be aware of his place in the long and enduring tradition of his calling, aware of the worthy seamen who have gone before him and of those, equally worthy, who will come after him. Such is Conrad's concept of the "craft" and of the credentials necessary to be included in the exclusive "fellowship."

Conrad's attitude toward seamen, particularly *his* seamen, is a bit complex. If his attitude toward the land and the sea is guarded and ambivalent and his attitude toward ships and toward the craft straightforward and unequivocal, his feelings toward seamen are a striking admixture of both. For the obviously worthy members of the fellowship, MacWhirr, Beard, Allistoun, for the strong-willed, indomitable men who are faint neither of heart nor foot and do their jobs without complaint, Conrad's admiration is boundless. On the other hand, for the Donkins, for the craven second mate of the *Nan-Shan,* for the officers of the *Patna,* for the misfits and miscasts who occasionally find their way aboard Conrad's ships and will never be members of the fellowship, his contempt is equally unmitigated.

There is a third group among Conrad's seamen, and here an attempt to arrive at Conrad's attitude is, at best, inconclusive. These are the men, essentially worthy, who doubt or who hesitate or who are unsure or who are, in Marlow's words, cursed with "soft spots." In these instances, Conrad wavers uncertainly between sympathy for and understanding of their shortcomings and the professional seaman's indignation, if not disdain, at their failure to measure up. And, in looking back over Conrad's sea tales, one final observation prompts itself. It is clearly these introspective men or these flawed men—the Jims, the Lingards, the Whalleys, the Brierlys, the captains of "The Secret Sharer" and *The Shadow-Line,* and even Marlow—who are the objects of Conrad's chief concern and with whom he is chiefly fascinated. But, thereby hangs a tale, and another book.

INDEX

AF